The Complete PANDAS/PANS Parent Handbook

What to Do When Your Child Develops Sudden OCD, Tics, or Behavior Changes

Willie Rosaline Randall

Healthcare provider names mentioned are fictional unless referring to published research authors or with explicit permission. School names, locations, and other identifying details in examples have been changed or created to protect privacy.

While every effort has been made to ensure the accuracy of medical and scientific information presented, research in PANDAS/PANS continues to evolve. Readers should consult current medical literature and qualified healthcare providers for the most up-to-date information on diagnosis and treatment options.

The author and publisher shall not be liable for any loss of profit or any other commercial damages, including but not limited to special, incidental, consequential, or other damages arising from the use of information in this book.

ISBN: 978-1-7642471-8-4

Isohan Publishing

Table of Contents

Introduction: Understanding PANDAS/PANS

If your child suddenly developed severe obsessive-compulsive behaviors overnight, would you know what was happening? What if they went from being your happy, well-adjusted kid to someone who couldn't touch doorknobs, had violent outbursts, or refused to eat anything but three specific foods? Most parents wouldn't connect these dramatic changes to something as simple as a strep throat infection.

Yet that's exactly what happens with PANDAS and PANS - conditions that can transform children almost instantly, leaving families bewildered and desperate for answers. You're not imagining things, and you're not alone in feeling lost when your child's personality seems to disappear overnight.

What Are PANDAS and PANS? Defining the Conditions

PANDAS stands for Pediatric Autoimmune Neuropsychiatric Disorders Associated with Streptococcal Infections. Think of it as your child's immune system getting confused after fighting off a strep infection and accidentally attacking healthy brain tissue instead (Swedo et al., 1998). The result? Sudden, severe psychiatric symptoms that seem to come out of nowhere.

PANS, or Pediatric Acute-onset Neuropsychiatric Syndrome, is the broader umbrella term. While PANDAS specifically links to strep infections, PANS can be triggered by various infections, environmental factors, or even unknown causes (Chang et al., 2015). Both conditions share that hallmark feature: the sudden, dramatic onset of psychiatric symptoms in previously healthy children.

Here's what makes these conditions so distinctive: Your child doesn't gradually develop anxiety or obsessive thoughts over months or years. Instead, they wake up one morning - or you pick them up from school one afternoon - and they're different. Completely different. The change is so stark that many parents can pinpoint the exact day their child's symptoms began.

Sarah, a mother from Oregon, describes it perfectly: "It was like someone flipped a switch. On Monday, Emma was my normal 8-year-old who loved playing with friends. By Friday, she couldn't leave her room without checking the door lock exactly seven times. She hadn't shown any signs of anxiety before that week."

These aren't typical childhood quirks or developmental phases. PANDAS and PANS represent a medical emergency disguised as psychiatric problems. The symptoms are real, the distress is genuine, and the underlying cause is biological - not psychological.

The Infection-Autoimmune Connection Explained

Your immune system is like a highly trained security force protecting your body from invaders. Normally, it does an excellent job identifying threats and eliminating them while leaving healthy tissue alone. But sometimes, this system makes a critical error.

Molecular mimicry is the scientific term for what goes wrong in PANDAS and PANS. Certain infections create proteins that look remarkably similar to proteins found in brain tissue, particularly in areas controlling movement, behavior, and cognition (Kirvan et al., 2003). When your child's immune system creates antibodies to fight the infection, some of these antibodies can't tell the difference between the invading germs and healthy brain cells.

Imagine giving a security guard a photo of a suspect, but the photo is so blurry that they end up arresting everyone who remotely resembles the person. That's essentially what happens in your child's brain. The antibodies meant to fight strep throat or other infections start attacking neurons in the basal ganglia - the brain region responsible for movement control and behavior regulation.

Research from the National Institute of Mental Health has identified specific brain regions affected by these rogue antibodies (Swedo et al., 2012). The caudate nucleus, putamen, and other structures in the basal ganglia become inflamed, disrupting normal neurotransmitter function. This inflammation explains why symptoms can be so severe and why they often involve movement disorders, compulsions, and behavioral changes.

The timing makes sense when you understand this process. Most parents report their child's symptoms beginning 1-6 weeks after an infection - exactly the timeframe needed for the immune system to mount a full antibody response and for those antibodies to cross the blood-brain barrier and cause inflammation.

But here's what many families don't realize: the original infection doesn't have to be severe or even noticeable. Some children develop PANDAS after mild strep throat that parents barely noticed. Others might have been exposed to strep from a sibling or classmate without ever showing typical strep symptoms themselves.

Why Traditional Approaches Often Fail

When parents first seek help for their child's sudden psychiatric symptoms, they usually end up in the wrong system entirely. Pediatricians, unfamiliar with PANDAS/PANS, often refer families to mental health professionals. Psychiatrists and psychologists, trained to view behavioral problems through a psychological lens, typically begin standard psychiatric treatment.

This creates a frustrating cycle: Your child receives therapy for obsessive-compulsive disorder, anxiety medications for panic attacks, or behavioral interventions for rage episodes. These treatments might provide modest improvement, but they're addressing symptoms rather than the underlying autoimmune inflammation causing those symptoms.

Traditional psychiatric medications often work differently - or don't work at all - in children with PANDAS/PANS (Frankovich et al., 2015). Selective serotonin reuptake inhibitors (SSRIs), commonly prescribed for OCD and anxiety, may actually worsen symptoms in some children with these conditions. Stimulant medications for attention problems can increase agitation and tics.

The diagnostic criteria for standard psychiatric conditions don't account for sudden onset. Most mental health conditions develop gradually over months or years. When a child meets criteria for OCD, anxiety disorders, or attention deficit disorder, clinicians follow established treatment protocols without considering that the rapid onset might indicate a completely different underlying cause.

Many families spend months or even years cycling through different mental health professionals, medications, and therapies without significant improvement. Meanwhile, the autoimmune inflammation continues, sometimes worsening over time or recurring with each new infection.

Dr. Susan Swedo, who first identified PANDAS at the National Institute of Mental Health, has noted that the average time from symptom onset to proper diagnosis is often 2-3 years (Swedo et al., 2015). During this time, children suffer unnecessarily, families exhaust their resources, and the condition may become more entrenched and difficult to treat.

How This Book Will Help Your Family

This handbook takes a radically different approach. Instead of treating your child's symptoms as separate psychiatric problems, we'll help you understand them as manifestations of an underlying medical condition that requires targeted treatment.

You'll learn to become a detective in your child's care. We'll show you how to track patterns, document symptoms, and present compelling evidence to healthcare providers. Many parents discover they become the most knowledgeable person on their child's medical team when it comes to PANDAS/PANS - not because they want to, but because they have to.

The book is organized to follow your likely journey: from recognizing symptoms and getting diagnosed to implementing treatment and

4

managing long-term care. Each chapter builds on the previous one, but you can also jump to specific sections when you need immediate help with particular challenges.

We'll address the practical realities other resources often skip. How do you handle a child who suddenly refuses to go to school? What do you tell family members who think you're overreacting? How do you advocate with insurance companies that don't understand these conditions? What works when traditional behavioral strategies fail?

You'll find detailed treatment protocols that go beyond what most physicians can provide during brief appointments. We'll explain not just what treatments exist, but how to access them, what to expect, and how to modify approaches based on your child's response.

Most importantly, you'll learn that recovery is possible. While PANDAS and PANS can be devastating in their acute phases, many children do recover completely with appropriate treatment. Others learn to manage their symptoms effectively and go on to live full, successful lives.

A Message of Hope for Parents

Right now, you might feel like you're drowning. The child you knew seems to have disappeared, replaced by someone consumed with fears, compulsions, and behaviors that don't make sense. You've probably questioned your parenting, wondered if you somehow caused this, and felt helpless watching your child struggle.

Let's be clear about something: this is not your fault. PANDAS and PANS are medical conditions with biological causes. You didn't create this situation through your parenting choices, your child's diet, or anything else you did or didn't do. These conditions can affect children from any family background, regardless of socioeconomic status, parenting style, or previous mental health history.

The intensity of symptoms in PANDAS/PANS can be frightening, but remember that intensity often correlates with treatability. The dramatic onset that makes these conditions so disturbing also means they're often responsive to appropriate medical treatment. Children who develop psychiatric symptoms gradually over years may face longer treatment timelines than those whose symptoms appeared suddenly due to autoimmune inflammation.

You're going to become stronger than you think possible. Parents of children with PANDAS/PANS often develop remarkable advocacy skills, medical knowledge, and resilience. You'll learn to navigate complex medical systems, interpret research studies, and make treatment decisions with confidence. This isn't the journey you planned, but you'll be amazed by your own capabilities.

Many families find that dealing with PANDAS/PANS, while challenging, ultimately brings them closer together. You'll develop deeper empathy, stronger communication skills, and a clearer sense of what truly matters. Your child will learn they can overcome significant challenges and that their family will support them through anything.

Recovery stories are everywhere once you know where to look. Children who couldn't leave their houses due to contamination fears now play sports and attend sleepovers. Kids who had violent rages triggered by minor changes in routine now handle stress with remarkable maturity. Families who felt isolated and hopeless have found effective treatments and rebuilt their lives.

The road ahead has challenges, but you don't have to travel it alone. Thousands of families have walked this path before you, and many have emerged stronger on the other side. This book will serve as your guide, helping you make informed decisions and avoid common pitfalls while keeping hope alive for your child's recovery.

Your child is still in there. The infection and inflammation have temporarily hijacked their brain, but with proper treatment, that amazing kid you know and love will return. Hold onto that truth during the difficult days ahead, because your unwavering belief in their recovery will be one of the most powerful tools in their healing process.

Chapter 1: Recognizing the Symptoms

The phone call came at 2 PM on a Tuesday. "Your daughter is hiding under her desk and won't come out," the school nurse told Lisa. "She keeps saying the pencils are dirty and won't touch anything in the classroom." Just three days earlier, 10-year-old Maya had been student of the month. Now she was having a complete meltdown over ordinary school supplies.

This wasn't a gradual change. There were no warning signs, no months of increasing anxiety, no family stressors that could explain such a dramatic shift. Maya had gone from a confident, social child to someone paralyzed by contamination fears almost overnight. The speed of this transformation is exactly what makes PANDAS/PANS so distinctive - and so often missed by healthcare providers unfamiliar with these conditions.

The Hallmark of Sudden, Dramatic Onset

The defining feature of PANDAS/PANS isn't any specific symptom - it's how quickly those symptoms appear. While typical psychiatric conditions develop gradually over months or years, PANDAS/PANS creates dramatic changes in days or weeks. Most parents can identify not just the week, but often the exact day their child's symptoms began.

Research indicates that 74% of children with PANDAS/PANS develop symptoms within 30 days of an infection, with many showing changes within just a few days (Murphy et al., 2015). This rapid onset occurs because the autoimmune response that triggers symptoms happens quickly once antibodies begin attacking brain tissue.

You might notice the change in several ways:

Your child wakes up one morning acting completely different than they did the night before. Teachers call because your previously well-behaved student is having behavioral problems at school. Family members comment that your child "seems off" or "not like

7

themselves." The change is so noticeable that even casual acquaintances pick up on it.

Take Jennifer's experience with her 7-year-old son Marcus. "On Sunday, he played happily with his cousins all afternoon. By Tuesday, he couldn't sit still for five minutes and was having meltdowns over things that never bothered him before. I actually thought someone must have done something to him because the change was so extreme."

This sudden onset often confuses parents because it doesn't match their understanding of mental health conditions. You might think, "Kids don't just develop OCD overnight," or "Anxiety disorders take time to develop." You're absolutely right about typical psychiatric conditions - which is exactly why PANDAS/PANS should be considered when dramatic symptoms appear suddenly.

The intensity of initial symptoms can be overwhelming. Unlike gradual psychiatric conditions where symptoms start mild and slowly worsen, PANDAS/PANS often begins with severe symptoms that disrupt daily functioning immediately. Children might go from no anxiety to being unable to leave their rooms, or from typical childhood behavior to having violent outbursts triggered by minor changes.

Core Symptoms: OCD, Tics, Anxiety, and Rage

Obsessive-compulsive behaviors are the most common presenting symptom, affecting up to 96% of children with PANDAS/PANS (Frankovich et al., 2015). But these aren't the mild perfectionist tendencies or preferences for order that many children display. We're talking about true compulsions that interfere with daily functioning.

Your child might suddenly need to check locks repeatedly before feeling safe, wash their hands until they're raw, or arrange objects in specific patterns before they can move on to other activities. They may develop elaborate bedtime rituals that take hours to complete, or become unable to wear certain clothes because they "feel wrong."

Contamination fears often dominate the obsessive-compulsive presentations. Children who previously played outside without concern suddenly can't touch doorknobs, refuse to use public restrooms, or insist on using paper towels to touch common surfaces. Some develop fears so severe they won't hug family members or sit on furniture others have used.

Tics and movement disorders appear in approximately 70% of children with PANDAS/PANS. These can include vocal tics like throat clearing, sniffing, or repeating words or phrases, as well as motor tics such as eye blinking, head jerking, or shoulder shrugging (Singer et al., 2012). Unlike temporary tic disorders that wax and wane gradually, PANDAS/PANS tics often appear suddenly and can be quite severe initially.

Anxiety symptoms go far beyond normal childhood worries. Children develop intense separation anxiety, refusing to let parents out of their sight even to use the bathroom. They may become terrified of situations they previously handled easily, like riding in cars, being in crowded places, or sleeping alone. Panic attacks can occur multiple times daily, with physical symptoms like rapid heartbeat, sweating, and difficulty breathing.

Rage episodes are among the most disturbing symptoms for families to witness. These aren't typical temper tantrums that children outgrow or learn to control. PANDAS/PANS rage can be explosive, unpredictable, and completely disproportionate to any trigger. A child might have a violent meltdown because their sandwich was cut in triangles instead of squares, or because someone moved their backpack.

During these episodes, children often seem to lose complete control. They may hit, kick, throw objects, or say things that are completely out of character. The rage can last for hours, leaving both the child and family emotionally exhausted. Many parents describe feeling like they're walking on eggshells, never knowing what might trigger the next explosion.

9

Secondary Symptoms: Sleep Disturbances, Regression, Food Restrictions

Sleep problems affect nearly every child with PANDAS/PANS, though they're often overlooked because families focus on the more dramatic daytime symptoms. Your child might suddenly develop severe insomnia, lying awake for hours despite being exhausted. Others experience frequent nightmares or night terrors that weren't present before symptom onset.

Some children develop elaborate bedtime rituals that must be completed perfectly before they can sleep. They might need to check that doors are locked multiple times, arrange stuffed animals in specific positions, or have parents repeat certain phrases. These rituals can take hours to complete and may need to be restarted if interrupted.

Bedwetting can return in children who have been dry for years. This regression often causes significant shame and embarrassment, particularly in older children. The bedwetting typically resolves as other PANDAS/PANS symptoms improve with treatment.

Academic and developmental regression can be striking. Previously successful students suddenly struggle with tasks they mastered long ago. Handwriting deteriorates dramatically - some children go from neat cursive to barely legible printing. Math skills that were automatic require tremendous effort. Reading comprehension drops significantly.

The regression extends beyond academics. Older children might start talking in baby voices, asking for help with tasks they can usually do independently, or wanting comfort items they had outgrown. This isn't attention-seeking behavior - the neuroinflammation genuinely affects cognitive and emotional development.

Food restrictions and eating problems develop in about 60% of children with PANDAS/PANS. Some children drastically limit their food choices, eating only a few "safe" foods. Others develop contamination fears about food, worrying about germs or foreign objects in their meals. Textures that never bothered them before become intolerable.

Weight loss can be rapid and concerning. Children might refuse entire food groups or become so anxious about eating that they consume very little throughout the day. Some develop ritualistic eating behaviors, like cutting food into specific shapes or eating items in a particular order.

Age-Related Presentation Differences

Younger children (ages 3-7) often present with more obvious behavioral symptoms. They may have dramatic tantrums, become extremely clingy, or develop intense fears of everyday objects or situations. Regressive behaviors like thumb sucking, baby talk, or toileting accidents are common in this age group.

Tics in younger children are often more noticeable and disruptive. They might develop loud vocal tics, repetitive movements that interfere with activities, or complex behavioral patterns they feel compelled to perform. Younger children also have more difficulty articulating their internal experiences, so obsessive thoughts might manifest as behavioral inflexibility or distress when routines change.

School-age children (ages 8-12) typically present with classic OCD symptoms that are easier for adults to recognize. They can often describe their obsessive thoughts and explain their compulsive behaviors, though they may feel embarrassed about them. Academic regression is usually more apparent in this age group because school demands are higher.

These children often develop social problems as their symptoms become noticeable to peers. They might avoid school activities, lose friendships, or become targets for teasing because of their unusual behaviors. The gap between their intellectual understanding that their behaviors are irrational and their inability to stop them can cause significant distress.

Adolescents (ages 13-18) may present with symptoms that look more like traditional psychiatric conditions. Depression, anxiety, and eating disorders are common presentations in this age group. However, the sudden onset still distinguishes PANDAS/PANS from typical adolescent mental health issues.

Teenagers often have more insight into their symptoms but also more shame about them. They may try to hide their compulsions or avoid situations where their symptoms might be noticeable. Academic pressure is typically highest in this age group, making any cognitive difficulties particularly problematic.

Red Flags That Distinguish PANDAS/PANS from Typical Childhood Issues

The sudden onset remains the most important distinguishing feature. Typical childhood anxiety, OCD, or tics develop gradually and often have identifiable triggers or precipitating factors. PANDAS/PANS symptoms appear rapidly and are often the first psychiatric symptoms the child has ever experienced.

Symptom severity is usually disproportionate to any apparent triggers. A child with typical anxiety might worry about a specific situation, like an upcoming test or social event. A child with PANDAS/PANS might develop paralyzing fears about everyday activities they previously enjoyed.

Multiple symptom domains appearing simultaneously is another red flag. It's unusual for children to suddenly develop OCD, tics, and severe anxiety all at once unless there's an underlying medical cause. PANDAS/PANS typically affects multiple areas of functioning simultaneously.

Physical symptoms often accompany the psychiatric presentation. Joint pain, frequent urination, dilated pupils, and deteriorated handwriting are common in PANDAS/PANS but not typically seen with primary psychiatric conditions (Frankovich et al., 2015).

Lack of response to standard treatments should raise suspicion. If your child isn't improving with appropriate psychiatric treatment after several months, consider whether an underlying medical condition might be present.

Parent Observations vs. Clinical Assessments

Your observations as a parent are invaluable and often more accurate than brief clinical assessments. You know your child's baseline behavior, personality, and capabilities better than any healthcare provider. Trust your instincts when something seems dramatically different.

Healthcare providers typically see children for brief appointments when symptoms might be controlled or less apparent. Many children with PANDAS/PANS can "hold it together" during short medical visits, only to fall apart once they return home. Your detailed observations of daily functioning provide crucial diagnostic information.

Start documenting everything immediately. Keep a detailed log of symptoms, their timing, and any potential triggers. Note the date symptoms began, what was happening in your child's life around that time, and any illnesses or exposures that preceded the onset. This documentation will be essential for getting proper diagnosis and treatment.

Take videos when possible, particularly of tics, compulsive behaviors, or rage episodes. Many healthcare providers have limited experience with PANDAS/PANS and may not fully understand the severity of symptoms based on verbal descriptions alone. Visual documentation can be powerfully persuasive.

Track patterns and triggers. Does your child have more symptoms at certain times of day? Do symptoms worsen with stress, illness, or changes in routine? Are there environmental factors that seem to help or hinder their functioning? These patterns can provide important clues about underlying mechanisms and effective treatments.

Real Families' Recognition Stories

The Thompson Family: Eight-year-old Jake had always been an easy-going child who loved school and playing with friends. After a mild case of strep throat in February, his parents noticed he seemed more irritable than usual. Within two weeks, Jake was having multiple daily meltdowns, couldn't concentrate on homework, and developed a fear of germs so severe he wouldn't touch anything without washing his hands afterward.

"I kept thinking he was just stressed about something at school," his mother recalls. "But when he started having panic attacks about using pencils because they might be dirty, I knew something was seriously wrong. This wasn't my child."

The family spent six months seeing various specialists before a psychiatrist familiar with PANDAS suggested testing for streptococcal antibodies. Jake's levels were significantly elevated, and he responded dramatically to antibiotic treatment combined with anti-inflammatory medications.

The Martinez Family: Twelve-year-old Sofia went from being an honor roll student to failing multiple classes within a month. She developed severe separation anxiety, couldn't sleep alone, and began performing elaborate checking rituals before leaving any room. Her parents initially attributed the changes to starting middle school.

"Everyone told us it was normal adolescent adjustment issues," Sofia's father explains. "But the change was so extreme and happened so fast. She went from confident and independent to needing constant reassurance about everything."

Sofia's symptoms began three weeks after a family camping trip where several children developed what seemed like minor cold symptoms. It wasn't until Sofia developed obvious tics that her pediatrician suggested PANDAS/PANS evaluation. Testing revealed evidence of recent mycoplasma infection, and Sofia improved significantly with targeted antibiotic therapy.

14

The Chen Family: Five-year-old David suddenly became violent and aggressive after what his parents thought was a stomach bug. He began hitting other children at preschool, having explosive tantrums at home, and developed food restrictions so severe he would only eat three specific foods.

"The school wanted us to see a behavioral specialist because they thought he had conduct disorder," his mother remembers. "But this behavior came out of nowhere. David had never been aggressive before."

The family's pediatrician initially dismissed their concerns, suggesting the behavior was attention-seeking. However, when David also developed significant sleep problems and began having accidents despite being potty-trained for two years, his parents insisted on further evaluation. Comprehensive testing revealed evidence of recent streptococcal infection, and David responded well to a combination of antibiotics and anti-inflammatory treatment.

Key Takeaways for Parents:

- Trust your instincts when your child's behavior changes dramatically and suddenly

- Document everything: timing, symptoms, potential triggers, and your child's baseline functioning

- The sudden onset of multiple psychiatric symptoms simultaneously should always raise suspicion for PANDAS/PANS

- Don't accept dismissive explanations when the changes are severe and rapid

- Video documentation can be invaluable for healthcare providers unfamiliar with these conditions

- Recovery is possible with appropriate recognition and treatmen

Chapter 2: The Diagnostic Journey

Walking into Dr. Peterson's office, Maria felt a mixture of hope and dread. This was their fourth specialist in six months, and 9-year-old Carlos was getting worse. His obsessive-compulsive behaviors had expanded from hand-washing to elaborate rituals that consumed hours each day. The tics that started three months ago were now so severe that other children stared at him in public.

"Has he always had anxiety?" Dr. Peterson asked, barely looking up from his computer screen. Maria wanted to scream. No, he hadn't always had anxiety. He'd gone from a happy, outgoing child to someone who couldn't leave the house without performing complex checking rituals. But she'd learned that most doctors didn't believe children could change so dramatically, so quickly.

This scenario plays out in medical offices across the country every day. Parents who know something is seriously wrong with their child find themselves in a medical system that wasn't designed to recognize or treat PANDAS/PANS. Getting an accurate diagnosis often requires persistence, preparation, and sometimes a willingness to challenge medical authorities who may be unfamiliar with these conditions.

Why Diagnosis Is Challenging: Lack of Definitive Tests

There's no single blood test or brain scan that definitively diagnoses PANDAS/PANS. Unlike strep throat, which can be confirmed with a rapid test, or diabetes, which shows up clearly in blood sugar levels, PANDAS/PANS diagnosis relies primarily on clinical observation and meeting specific criteria. This uncertainty makes many healthcare providers uncomfortable and reluctant to make the diagnosis.

The closest thing to diagnostic testing involves measuring antibodies against brain tissue and streptococcal markers, but these tests aren't standardized across laboratories and results can be difficult to interpret (Moleculera Labs, 2018). Some children with clear PANDAS/PANS symptoms have normal antibody levels, while others with elevated antibodies don't meet all clinical criteria.

Most healthcare providers receive little or no training about PANDAS/PANS during medical school or residency. A 2016 survey found that only 34% of pediatricians were familiar with PANDAS diagnostic criteria, and fewer than 20% felt confident treating these conditions . This knowledge gap means many families encounter skepticism or dismissal when they suggest PANDAS/PANS as a possible explanation for their child's symptoms.

The psychiatric community has been particularly slow to accept PANDAS/PANS as valid diagnoses. Many mental health professionals view sudden-onset psychiatric symptoms through a psychological rather than medical lens, focusing on environmental stressors or family dynamics rather than biological causes. This perspective can delay appropriate medical treatment for months or years.

Insurance companies often compound diagnostic challenges by refusing to cover PANDAS/PANS-related testing or treatment. Many insurers consider these conditions "experimental" or "unproven," despite growing research evidence and acceptance by major medical institutions like Stanford University and the National Institute of Mental Health.

Finding Knowledgeable Healthcare Providers

Start by contacting PANDAS/PANS organizations for provider referrals. The PANDAS Physicians Network maintains a list of healthcare providers experienced in diagnosing and treating these conditions. While this list isn't comprehensive, it's an excellent starting point for finding knowledgeable clinicians in your area.

Look for providers who specialize in pediatric autoimmune conditions, integrative medicine, or functional medicine approaches. These specialists are often more familiar with PANDAS/PANS and more willing to consider immune-mediated causes of psychiatric symptoms. Some infectious disease specialists, particularly those who work with children, have experience with these conditions.

Don't overlook nurse practitioners and physician assistants. Many advanced practice providers have more time to spend with patients and may be more willing to investigate unusual presentations. Some of the most knowledgeable PANDAS/PANS clinicians are nurse practitioners who have developed expertise through treating numerous affected children.

Research potential providers before scheduling appointments. Check their websites, read patient reviews, and call their offices to ask about their experience with PANDAS/PANS. Some providers advertise their expertise in these conditions, while others may have experience but don't specifically mention it online.

Be prepared to travel for expert evaluation. Many families find they need to go outside their immediate geographic area to find experienced providers. While this can be expensive and logistically challenging, getting proper diagnosis and treatment recommendations from an expert can save time and money in the long run.

Consider telemedicine consultations with specialists who don't practice in your area. Many experienced PANDAS/PANS providers offer virtual consultations for initial evaluations or treatment planning. While they can't perform physical examinations remotely, they can review your documentation and provide valuable guidance.

Preparing for Appointments: Documentation Strategies

Create a comprehensive timeline of your child's symptoms. Start with their baseline functioning and personality before symptoms began. Include specific dates when possible, particularly the onset of psychiatric symptoms and any preceding illnesses or stressors. Note how symptoms have progressed or changed over time.

Document all treatments attempted and your child's response to each intervention. Include medications (with doses and duration), therapy approaches, and any complementary treatments you've tried. Note both improvements and adverse reactions, as patterns of treatment response can provide diagnostic clues.

Compile medical records from all providers who have evaluated your child. This includes pediatricians, specialists, emergency room visits, and mental health professionals. Having complete records prevents redundant testing and helps new providers understand the diagnostic journey you've already undertaken.

Take videos of symptoms whenever possible, particularly tics, compulsive behaviors, or rage episodes. Many symptoms fluctuate throughout the day or may not be apparent during brief medical appointments. Video documentation provides objective evidence of symptom severity and characteristics.

Prepare a list of specific questions and concerns. Medical appointments can be overwhelming, and it's easy to forget important topics you wanted to discuss. Write down your questions beforehand and don't hesitate to refer to your notes during the appointment.

Bring a support person when possible. Having another adult present can help you remember important information discussed during the appointment and provide emotional support during what can be a stressful process.

The PANDAS/PANS Diagnostic Criteria

PANDAS diagnostic criteria include five specific requirements: abrupt onset of obsessive-compulsive disorder and/or tics, prepubertal symptom onset, episodic course with dramatic symptom exacerbations, association with group A streptococcal infection, and neurological abnormalities during symptom exacerbations (Swedo et al., 2012).

The **abrupt onset** requirement distinguishes PANDAS from typical psychiatric conditions that develop gradually. Symptoms must appear suddenly, usually within 24-72 hours, rather than emerging slowly over weeks or months. This dramatic onset is often the most compelling evidence supporting the diagnosis.

Prepubertal onset was originally required for PANDAS diagnosis, but many experts now recognize that these conditions can affect adolescents and even adults. The PANS criteria removed the age restriction while maintaining the requirement for sudden symptom onset.

PANS diagnostic criteria are broader and more inclusive. They require abrupt onset of obsessive-compulsive or food restriction behaviors plus two additional symptoms from a specific list: anxiety, emotional lability, depression, irritability, behavioral regression, academic decline, sensory abnormalities, or somatic complaints (Chang et al., 2015).

The **episodic course** refers to the pattern of symptom exacerbations and improvements that many children experience. Symptoms may worsen during infections or stressful periods and improve between episodes. Some children have a single severe episode followed by complete recovery, while others experience multiple relapses.

Neurological abnormalities can include tics, choreiform movements, handwriting changes, or other motor symptoms. These signs suggest brain involvement and support the autoimmune hypothesis underlying PANDAS/PANS.

Common Diagnostic Obstacles and How to Overcome Them

"Your child is too young for OCD" is a common misconception among healthcare providers. While OCD typically begins in adolescence or early adulthood, PANDAS/PANS can cause severe obsessive-compulsive symptoms in very young children. Point out that the sudden onset and severity distinguish these symptoms from typical childhood development.

"Children don't develop psychiatric symptoms overnight" reflects unfamiliarity with autoimmune causes of mental health problems. Educate providers about the growing research on immune-mediated psychiatric conditions and provide references to peer-reviewed articles supporting PANDAS/PANS as valid diagnoses.

"These symptoms are probably due to stress" dismisses the biological nature of PANDAS/PANS. While stress can trigger symptom exacerbations, it doesn't explain the sudden onset or specific symptom constellation seen in these conditions. Emphasize that your child had no significant stressors preceding symptom onset.

"Let's try standard psychiatric treatment first" delays appropriate medical intervention. While psychiatric treatments may provide some symptom relief, they don't address the underlying autoimmune inflammation. Request evaluation for potential medical causes before beginning lengthy psychiatric treatment trials.

Providers who are dismissive or resistant to considering PANDAS/PANS may simply lack knowledge about these conditions. Bring educational materials to appointments and offer to share resources with providers who seem interested in learning more. However, don't waste time trying to educate providers who are hostile or completely closed to considering these diagnoses.

Second Opinions: When and How to Seek Them

Seek a second opinion if your current provider: dismisses your concerns without adequate evaluation, refuses to consider PANDAS/PANS despite clear symptom patterns, wants to begin extensive psychiatric treatment without ruling out medical causes, or makes you feel like you're overreacting to legitimate concerns about your child.

The timing of second opinions matters. If your child's symptoms are severe and interfering significantly with daily functioning, don't wait months for standard psychiatric treatment to work. Early intervention in PANDAS/PANS often leads to better outcomes, so seeking expert evaluation sooner rather than later is usually beneficial.

When requesting second opinions, be honest about your concerns with current care. Explain that you want to ensure all possible causes have been considered before pursuing long-term psychiatric treatment. Most reasonable healthcare providers will support your desire for thorough evaluation.

Prepare thoroughly for second opinion appointments. Compile all relevant medical records, create detailed symptom timelines, and document your child's response to any treatments attempted. Second opinion providers need comprehensive information to make informed recommendations.

Consider seeking second opinions from different types of specialists. If your pediatrician isn't helpful, try a pediatric neurologist or immunologist. If psychiatrists dismiss medical causes, consult with integrative medicine physicians who take a broader approach to chronic symptoms.

Insurance Considerations and Advocacy

Contact your insurance company before pursuing PANDAS/PANS evaluation to understand coverage limitations and prior authorization requirements. Many insurers require documentation of failed standard treatments before approving specialized testing or treatments.

Document all communications with insurance companies in writing. Follow up phone conversations with emails summarizing what was discussed and any commitments made by insurance representatives. Keep detailed records of claim numbers, representative names, and dates of all interactions.

Appeal denied claims with additional documentation and provider support. Many initial denials are overturned on appeal, particularly when accompanied by letters from treating physicians explaining medical necessity. Don't accept the first denial as final.

Work with your healthcare provider's billing department to ensure claims are submitted with appropriate diagnostic codes and supporting documentation. Experienced PANDAS/PANS providers often have staff who understand insurance requirements for these conditions.

Consider hiring a healthcare advocate if insurance battles become overwhelming. Professional advocates understand insurance systems and can often achieve better outcomes than families trying to navigate complex appeals processes alone.

Out-of-network providers may be necessary for expert PANDAS/PANS care. While this increases out-of-pocket costs, it may be worth the expense to get accurate diagnosis and treatment recommendations. Some families find that effective treatment from out-of-network specialists ultimately costs less than years of ineffective treatments covered by insurance.

Key Takeaways for Your Diagnostic Journey:

- Diagnosis relies primarily on clinical criteria rather than definitive tests, making provider knowledge crucial

- Thorough documentation of symptoms, timeline, and treatment responses strengthens your case

- Don't accept dismissive responses from providers unfamiliar with PANDAS/PANS

- Second opinions are often necessary and can prevent months of ineffective treatment

- Insurance advocacy requires persistence, documentation, and sometimes professional help

- Expert evaluation, even if expensive, often saves time and money in the long run

- Trust your parental instincts - you know your child better than any healthcare provider

Chapter 3: Differential Diagnosis

Dr. Williams looked across her desk at the exhausted parents sitting with their 11-year-old daughter Emma. "I understand you're concerned about PANDAS," she said carefully, "but we need to make sure we're not missing other possibilities. Emma's symptoms could have several different explanations."

This conversation happens in medical offices every day, and it reflects good medical practice. Skilled clinicians know that jumping to conclusions, even appealing ones, can lead to missed diagnoses and inappropriate treatment. But for parents desperate for answers, the differential diagnosis process can feel like an endless series of roadblocks preventing their child from getting help.

The reality is that thorough evaluation benefits everyone. Some children initially thought to have PANDAS/PANS actually have other treatable conditions. Others may have PANDAS/PANS plus additional medical problems that need attention. And occasionally, children have conditions that mimic PANDAS/PANS so closely that even experienced specialists need time and testing to sort things out.

Conditions That Mimic PANDAS/PANS

Sydenham's chorea is probably the condition most similar to PANDAS/PANS, which makes sense because both involve autoimmune reactions to streptococcal infections affecting the brain. Children with Sydenham's chorea develop involuntary movements, emotional instability, and sometimes obsessive-compulsive behaviors after rheumatic fever .

The key difference is that Sydenham's chorea typically includes prominent movement abnormalities - jerky, uncontrollable movements of the face, hands, or entire body. PANDAS/PANS can include subtle movement problems, but dramatic chorea movements are uncommon. Additionally, Sydenham's chorea usually occurs after more severe streptococcal infections that cause rheumatic fever, while PANDAS/PANS can follow mild or even asymptomatic strep exposure.

Autoimmune encephalitis represents a broader category of conditions where immune reactions cause brain inflammation. Anti-NMDA receptor encephalitis, for example, can cause psychiatric symptoms, movement disorders, and cognitive problems that overlap significantly with PANDAS/PANS presentations (Graus et al., 2016).

These conditions often begin more gradually than PANDAS/PANS and may include additional neurological symptoms like seizures, severe memory problems, or altered consciousness. However, some cases of autoimmune encephalitis can present with primarily psychiatric symptoms, making differentiation challenging without specialized testing.

Tourette syndrome and chronic tic disorders share the movement abnormalities seen in many PANDAS/PANS cases. However, typical tic disorders develop gradually over months or years, with tics waxing and waning in severity. The sudden onset of severe tics in PANDAS/PANS, often accompanied by obsessive-compulsive behaviors and other psychiatric symptoms, helps distinguish these conditions.

Some children may have underlying genetic predisposition to tics that becomes activated by the immune response in PANDAS/PANS. These cases can be particularly complex to diagnose and treat, as they may require approaches targeting both the autoimmune inflammation and the underlying tic disorder.

Wilson's disease is a genetic condition affecting copper metabolism that can cause psychiatric symptoms, movement disorders, and cognitive problems. While much rarer than PANDAS/PANS, Wilson's disease can present during childhood or adolescence with symptoms that overlap significantly with autoimmune neuropsychiatric conditions .

The gradual onset and presence of liver abnormalities or characteristic eye changes (Kayser-Fleischer rings) help distinguish

Wilson's disease. However, psychiatric symptoms may be the first manifestation, making testing for Wilson's disease important in cases where PANDAS/PANS diagnosis is uncertain.

Standard Psychiatric Conditions vs. Autoimmune Presentations

Primary obsessive-compulsive disorder typically begins gradually, with symptoms slowly increasing in frequency and intensity over months or years. Children often try to hide their symptoms initially, and parents may not notice problems until they become severe. In contrast, PANDAS/PANS OCD appears suddenly and is usually obvious to everyone around the child.

The content of obsessions and compulsions can also differ. PANDAS/PANS often involves contamination fears, symmetry obsessions, and aggressive or sexual thoughts that are particularly disturbing to young children. Primary OCD in children more commonly involves fears about harm coming to loved ones or excessive concern about doing things "just right."

Generalized anxiety disorder develops slowly as children begin worrying excessively about multiple life domains. The anxiety in PANDAS/PANS tends to be more specific - often related to contamination, separation, or changes in routine - and appears abruptly rather than building gradually over time.

Children with primary anxiety disorders usually respond predictably to standard treatments like cognitive-behavioral therapy and selective serotonin reuptake inhibitors. Those with PANDAS/PANS may have paradoxical reactions to these treatments, with some children becoming more agitated or developing new symptoms.

Attention deficit hyperactivity disorder (ADHD) symptoms typically become apparent gradually as academic and social demands increase. Parents often report that their child "has always been hyperactive" or "never could sit still." PANDAS/PANS can cause attention and hyperactivity problems, but these appear suddenly in previously focused children.

The distractibility in PANDAS/PANS often relates to intrusive thoughts or compulsions rather than true attention deficits. Children may appear inattentive because they're performing mental rituals or trying to resist obsessive thoughts, not because they have primary attention problems.

Major depression in children usually develops over weeks or months, often triggered by identifiable stressors or life changes. While PANDAS/PANS can cause mood symptoms, these typically occur alongside obsessive-compulsive behaviors, tics, or other characteristic symptoms rather than in isolation.

The irritability and emotional lability in PANDAS/PANS can be explosive and unpredictable, different from the persistent sadness or hopelessness typical of primary depression. Additionally, mood symptoms in PANDAS/PANS often fluctuate dramatically from day to day or even hour to hour.

Medical Conditions to Rule Out

Thyroid disorders can cause anxiety, hyperactivity, sleep problems, and behavioral changes that overlap with PANDAS/PANS symptoms. Hyperthyroidism, in particular, can cause sudden onset of anxiety and agitation in children. Simple blood tests can rule out thyroid problems, making this an important early step in evaluation.

Both overactive and underactive thyroid conditions can affect mood, energy, and cognitive function. Thyroid dysfunction is relatively common in children and easily treatable, making it essential to test thyroid function in any child with sudden behavioral changes.

Lyme disease and other tick-borne infections can cause neuropsychiatric symptoms that mimic PANDAS/PANS. Some children develop anxiety, obsessive-compulsive behaviors, tics, and cognitive problems after Lyme disease infection. The geographic distribution of Lyme disease and history of tick exposure can provide important clues.

Testing for Lyme disease can be challenging because standard tests may miss early or chronic infections. Some specialists recommend more comprehensive testing panels for tick-borne diseases in children with PANDAS/PANS-like symptoms, particularly in areas where these infections are common.

Brain tumors, while rare, can occasionally cause psychiatric symptoms before other neurological signs become apparent. Tumors affecting the frontal lobe or basal ganglia might cause obsessive-compulsive behaviors, personality changes, or movement disorders.

The gradual progression typically seen with brain tumors differs from the sudden onset characteristic of PANDAS/PANS, but brain imaging may be recommended in cases where the diagnosis is uncertain or symptoms are particularly severe.

Seizure disorders sometimes present with behavioral or psychiatric symptoms rather than obvious convulsions. Complex partial seizures can cause periods of altered behavior, repetitive movements, or unusual thoughts that might be mistaken for psychiatric symptoms.

Electroencephalogram (EEG) testing can identify seizure activity, though normal EEGs don't completely rule out seizure disorders. Some children may need prolonged EEG monitoring or sleep-deprived studies to detect subtle seizure activity.

Substance use must be considered in adolescents presenting with sudden behavioral changes. While most parents don't suspect their children of using drugs, some substances can cause dramatic personality changes that might be mistaken for psychiatric conditions.

Drug testing and honest conversations about substance use are important parts of evaluation, particularly in teenagers. Some substances can trigger lasting psychiatric symptoms even after the drug has been eliminated from the body.

The Importance of Comprehensive Evaluation

Rushing to diagnosis can be as problematic as delaying appropriate treatment. While parents understandably want quick answers, thorough evaluation helps ensure children receive the most appropriate and effective treatment. Missing other medical conditions could delay proper treatment and potentially cause harm.

A comprehensive evaluation typically includes detailed medical history, physical examination, basic laboratory studies, and sometimes specialized testing based on the clinical presentation. The exact tests needed vary depending on the child's specific symptoms and medical history.

Laboratory studies usually include complete blood count, comprehensive metabolic panel, thyroid function tests, and inflammatory markers. Additional tests might include vitamin levels, autoimmune markers, or infectious disease studies depending on the clinical picture.

Some specialists recommend testing for specific autoantibodies associated with PANDAS/PANS, though these tests aren't standardized and results must be interpreted carefully. Elevated antibodies can support the diagnosis but normal levels don't rule out PANDAS/PANS.

Neuropsychological testing can help document cognitive changes and distinguish between different types of learning problems. Children with PANDAS/PANS often show specific patterns of cognitive difficulties that differ from other conditions affecting academic performance.

This testing can be particularly valuable for educational planning and documenting improvement with treatment. However, testing during acute symptom phases may not accurately reflect the child's true capabilities.

Working with Skeptical Healthcare Providers

Approach skeptical providers with patience and education rather than confrontation. Many healthcare providers genuinely want to help but may lack knowledge about PANDAS/PANS. Bringing educational materials and research articles can help bridge this knowledge gap.

Focus on the facts of your child's presentation rather than insisting on a specific diagnosis. Emphasize the sudden onset, severity of symptoms, and impact on functioning. These objective observations are harder to dismiss than requests for particular treatments.

Ask questions that highlight important clinical features: "Is it common for children to develop severe OCD overnight?" or "What might cause such dramatic behavioral changes in a previously healthy child?" This approach helps providers think through the differential diagnosis rather than feeling pressured to accept your conclusions.

Request specific explanations when providers dismiss PANDAS/PANS as a possibility. Ask what alternative diagnoses they're considering and how those conditions explain your child's particular symptom pattern. This forces more thorough clinical reasoning.

Be prepared to find new providers if necessary. While it's worth trying to educate skeptical healthcare providers, don't waste months with someone who refuses to consider all possibilities. Your child's health is too important to compromise for provider relationships.

When Multiple Conditions Coexist

Some children have PANDAS/PANS plus additional medical or psychiatric conditions. For example, a child might have underlying ADHD that becomes dramatically worse during a PANDAS/PANS episode. Or they might develop secondary depression from months of untreated OCD symptoms.

These complex cases require careful treatment planning that addresses all contributing factors. Treating only the PANDAS/PANS might not resolve all symptoms, while treating only the comorbid conditions ignores the underlying autoimmune inflammation.

Genetic factors may predispose some children to both autoimmune conditions and psychiatric disorders. Family history of autoimmune diseases, OCD, or tic disorders might increase the likelihood of developing PANDAS/PANS while also suggesting other risk factors to consider.

The timing of symptom development can provide clues about which conditions are primary versus secondary. Symptoms that appeared suddenly around the time of illness are more likely related to PANDAS/PANS, while longstanding problems probably represent separate conditions.

Treatment coordination becomes crucial when multiple conditions are present. Different medications might interact with each other, and some treatments effective for one condition might worsen another. Working with providers experienced in complex cases is often necessary.

Key Takeaways for Differential Diagnosis:

- Comprehensive evaluation protects against missing other treatable conditions

- The sudden onset remains the most distinguishing feature of PANDAS/PANS

- Some conditions require specific testing to rule out, particularly thyroid disorders and infectious diseases

- Multiple conditions can coexist, requiring complex treatment approaches

- Skeptical providers often respond better to education than confrontation

- Don't let the differential diagnosis process delay treatment indefinitely if PANDAS/PANS criteria are clearly met

- Seek experienced providers for complex cases involving multiple potential diagnoses

Chapter 4: Treatment Strategies - Addressing the Infection

The call came at 7 AM on a Saturday. Jennifer's voice was shaky as she told Dr. Martinez about her 10-year-old son Tyler. "The antibiotics aren't working anymore," she said. "His OCD symptoms came back full force after just three days off the medication. What do we do now?"

This scenario plays out in thousands of families dealing with PANDAS/PANS. The child shows dramatic improvement on antibiotics, giving everyone hope that recovery is finally within reach. Then the symptoms return, often worse than before, leaving parents wondering if they're fighting a losing battle against an invisible enemy.

Here's what Jennifer didn't know: treating the infectious component of PANDAS/PANS isn't as simple as taking antibiotics for a week and expecting permanent recovery. The relationship between infection, immune response, and neuropsychiatric symptoms is complex and often requires sustained, strategic treatment approaches that go far beyond standard antibiotic protocols.

Understanding the Infectious Triggers

Streptococcal bacteria remain the most well-documented trigger for PANDAS, but research has identified numerous other infectious agents that can precipitate similar autoimmune reactions. Group A Streptococcus (the bacteria causing strep throat) was the first identified culprit, but we now know that Group C and Group G streptococcal strains can also trigger symptoms (Murphy et al., 2015).

The infection doesn't have to be severe or even symptomatic to trigger PANDAS/PANS. Some children develop symptoms after exposure to strep bacteria without ever showing signs of sore throat, fever, or other typical strep symptoms. This silent exposure often occurs through family members, classmates, or community contacts who carry streptococcal bacteria.

Mycoplasma pneumoniae has emerged as another significant trigger, particularly for PANS cases. This atypical bacteria causes "walking pneumonia" and can persist in the body for months, creating ongoing immune stimulation. Unlike strep infections that tend to be acute and resolve quickly, mycoplasma infections often become chronic and may require extended treatment courses .

Other documented triggers include influenza viruses, Epstein-Barr virus, varicella (chickenpox), and various respiratory viruses. Some cases appear to be triggered by multiple infections occurring simultaneously or in rapid succession, overwhelming the child's immune system and triggering the autoimmune response.

Bacterial overgrowth in the gut may also contribute to ongoing symptoms in some children. The intestinal microbiome plays a crucial role in immune function, and disruptions can lead to systemic inflammation that perpetuates PANDAS/PANS symptoms even after the original infection has been cleared.

Research suggests that genetic factors influence which children develop PANDAS/PANS after infectious exposure. Certain genetic variations affecting immune function or blood-brain barrier permeability may predispose some children to autoimmune reactions while protecting others .

Antibiotic Protocols and Considerations

The goal of antibiotic treatment isn't just eliminating active infection - it's reducing the bacterial load that's driving ongoing immune stimulation. Many children with PANDAS/PANS don't have active infections when symptoms appear, but they may harbor persistent bacteria or have immune systems that remain hypervigilant against bacterial antigens.

Standard strep throat treatment typically involves 10 days of penicillin or amoxicillin. For PANDAS/PANS, many specialists recommend longer courses - often 30 to 90 days or more - to ensure complete bacterial eradication and allow the immune system to calm down (Swedo et al., 2017).

Azithromycin has become a preferred choice for many PANDAS/PANS specialists because of its anti-inflammatory properties in addition to antibiotic effects. The typical dose is 250-500mg daily (depending on the child's weight) for extended periods. Some children respond better to daily dosing, while others do well with three times weekly maintenance protocols.

For children with suspected or confirmed mycoplasma infections, longer courses of macrolide antibiotics (azithromycin, clarithromycin, or erythromycin) may be necessary. Mycoplasma is notoriously difficult to eradicate and often requires 6-12 weeks of treatment or longer.

Combination antibiotic therapy may be needed for children who don't respond to single agents. Some specialists combine a beta-lactam antibiotic (like amoxicillin) with a macrolide, targeting different bacterial populations and providing broader anti-inflammatory coverage.

The timing of antibiotic treatment can affect outcomes. Children treated within weeks of symptom onset often respond more dramatically than those who receive treatment months or years later. However, even children with chronic symptoms may benefit from appropriate antibiotic therapy.

Pulsed antibiotic protocols involve giving high-dose antibiotics for several days, followed by antibiotic-free periods. This approach may help prevent bacterial resistance while maintaining therapeutic benefits. Some children do better with continuous treatment, while others respond to pulsed regimens.

Antimicrobial Treatments Beyond Antibiotics

Antiviral medications may be appropriate for children whose PANDAS/PANS was triggered by viral infections. Acyclovir or valacyclovir might be used for herpes virus triggers, while oseltamivir could be considered for influenza-related cases. The evidence for antiviral treatment in PANDAS/PANS is limited, but some children show improvement.

Antifungal treatments deserve consideration, particularly in children with histories of recurrent yeast infections or significant antibiotic exposure. Candida overgrowth can contribute to systemic inflammation and may perpetuate PANDAS/PANS symptoms. Fluconazole, nystatin, or other antifungal agents might be beneficial in selected cases.

Probiotics and prebiotic supplements can help restore healthy gut bacteria after antibiotic treatment. High-quality, multi-strain probiotics containing Lactobacillus and Bifidobacterium species are typically recommended. Some children benefit from specific strains like Lactobacillus rhamnosus or Saccharomyces boulardii.

Herbal antimicrobials provide alternative options for children who can't tolerate conventional antibiotics or need additional antimicrobial support. Oil of oregano, berberine, and monolaurin have antimicrobial properties and may help reduce bacterial, viral, or fungal loads.

Colloidal silver, while controversial, has been used by some families as an antimicrobial agent. However, concerns about potential toxicity and lack of standardization make this approach risky without proper medical supervision.

Prophylactic Treatment Approaches

Prevention of new infections becomes crucial once a child has been diagnosed with PANDAS/PANS. Many children experience symptom flares with each new streptococcal exposure, making infection prevention a priority for maintaining stability.

Daily low-dose antibiotics can prevent recurrent strep infections in vulnerable children. Penicillin 250mg twice daily or azithromycin 250mg three times weekly are common prophylactic regimens. This approach is similar to rheumatic fever prevention protocols used in cardiology.

Family treatment may be necessary when household members are chronic strep carriers. Testing and treating family members, including parents and siblings, can eliminate ongoing exposure sources. Some families need to treat pets as well, since animals can occasionally carry streptococcal bacteria.

Aggressive treatment of any new infections is essential. Even minor respiratory infections should be treated promptly and aggressively to prevent symptom flares. Some families keep antibiotics on hand for immediate treatment when symptoms of new infections appear.

Environmental modifications can reduce infection risk. Regular handwashing, avoiding crowded places during flu season, and maintaining good hygiene practices help minimize exposure. Some families choose to limit activities during high-risk periods.

Immune system support through proper nutrition, adequate sleep, stress reduction, and appropriate supplementation may help children resist new infections. Vitamin D, zinc, and vitamin C are commonly recommended for immune support.

Managing Antibiotic Resistance and Side Effects

Extended antibiotic use raises legitimate concerns about resistance development. Working with infectious disease specialists or experienced PANDAS/PANS physicians helps balance treatment benefits against resistance risks. Some doctors rotate antibiotics periodically to minimize resistance development.

Monitoring for side effects becomes crucial during long-term antibiotic treatment. Common problems include gastrointestinal upset, yeast overgrowth, and disruption of normal bacterial flora. Some antibiotics can cause photosensitivity, requiring sun protection measures.

C. difficile infection represents a serious but rare complication of extended antibiotic use. Children who develop severe diarrhea, abdominal pain, or fever during antibiotic treatment need immediate medical evaluation. Probiotic supplementation may help prevent this complication.

Liver function monitoring may be necessary with certain antibiotics, particularly macrolides used for extended periods. Regular blood tests can detect early signs of liver irritation before serious problems develop.

Allergic reactions can develop during extended antibiotic courses, even in children who previously tolerated the same medications. New rashes, respiratory symptoms, or gastrointestinal problems may indicate allergic reactions requiring medication changes.

Some children develop antibiotic-associated behavioral changes, including increased hyperactivity, sleep problems, or mood changes. These effects are usually temporary but may require dosage adjustments or medication switches.

Monitoring Treatment Response

Symptom tracking becomes essential for evaluating antibiotic effectiveness. Many families use daily symptom rating scales to monitor improvements or deteriorations. Apps or simple paper logs can help track patterns over time.

The response to appropriate antibiotic treatment often follows predictable patterns. Many children show initial improvement within days to weeks, followed by gradual continued progress over months. Some experience temporary worsening before improvement, possibly due to bacterial die-off reactions.

Herxheimer reactions can occur when large numbers of bacteria are killed rapidly, releasing toxins that temporarily worsen symptoms. These reactions typically last 24-72 hours and may indicate that treatment is working. However, distinguishing Herxheimer reactions from treatment failure requires experience.

Laboratory monitoring may include periodic blood counts, liver function tests, and inflammatory markers. Some specialists track specific antibody levels to gauge treatment response, though these tests aren't standardized across all laboratories.

Functional improvements often lag behind symptom improvements. A child might show reduced OCD symptoms but still struggle with academic performance or social functioning. Complete recovery typically takes months and may require additional interventions beyond antibiotics.

Duration of Treatment Decisions

There's no standard duration for antibiotic treatment in PANDAS/PANS. Some children recover completely after 30-90 days of treatment, while others require maintenance therapy for months or years. Treatment duration should be individualized based on symptom response and risk factors.

Children who respond dramatically to initial antibiotic treatment often need extended courses to maintain improvements. Stopping antibiotics too early frequently leads to symptom recurrence, requiring retreatment and potentially longer recovery times.

Gradual antibiotic tapering may be preferable to abrupt discontinuation. Some children can transition from daily to every-other-day dosing, then to twice-weekly maintenance before eventually stopping treatment completely.

Seasonal considerations may influence treatment duration. Children who tend to have more infections during school year might benefit from prophylactic treatment during high-risk periods, with treatment breaks during summer months.

The decision to continue or discontinue antibiotics should balance symptom control, side effect risks, and resistance concerns. Regular reassessment with experienced providers helps optimize treatment decisions over time.

Some children require intermittent treatment courses rather than continuous therapy. These children might do well off antibiotics for months, then need retreatment during symptom flares or after new infections.

Success Stories from the Trenches

Consider the case of 8-year-old Emma, whose severe OCD symptoms disappeared within two weeks of starting azithromycin. Her parents wanted to stop the antibiotic after a month of treatment, but her doctor recommended continuing for three months. When they tried stopping at six weeks, Emma's symptoms returned within days. She ultimately needed five months of continuous treatment before successfully discontinuing antibiotics.

Twelve-year-old Marcus required a different approach. His symptoms responded partially to amoxicillin but didn't resolve completely until his doctor added azithromycin to target possible mycoplasma infection. The combination therapy for eight weeks led to complete symptom resolution that lasted after discontinuing both antibiotics.

Nine-year-old Sarah's family learned about the importance of family screening when her symptoms kept recurring despite appropriate antibiotic treatment. Testing revealed that her father was a chronic strep carrier. After treating the entire family, Sarah's symptoms stabilized and she was able to stop prophylactic antibiotics.

Key Principles for Success:

- Start with appropriate antibiotics based on likely infectious triggers

- Don't expect immediate results - improvement often takes weeks to months

- Extended treatment courses are usually necessary, unlike typical infections

- Monitor for side effects but don't stop effective treatment prematurely

- Consider combination therapy for partial responders

- Treat family members and eliminate infection sources

- Work with experienced providers who understand PANDAS/PANS treatment nuances

- Balance treatment benefits against risks through regular reassessment

Chapter 5: Modulating the Immune System

Rachel stared at the prescription bottle in her hands, reading "Prednisone" for the third time. Her 7-year-old daughter Mia had been suffering from severe PANDAS symptoms for four months. Antibiotics had helped some, but the OCD and tics were still disrupting every aspect of their family life. "Steroids?" she asked Dr. Chen. "For psychiatric symptoms?"

"Think of it this way," Dr. Chen explained. "If Mia had severe asthma, you wouldn't hesitate to use anti-inflammatory medication to help her breathe. Her brain inflammation is just as real as lung inflammation - we just can't see it as easily."

This conversation happens frequently in PANDAS/PANS treatment because parents understandably worry about giving powerful medications to children with "behavioral problems." But **the key insight is that these aren't behavioral problems at all - they're medical symptoms of brain inflammation that often require medical interventions to resolve.**

Anti-inflammatory Approaches and NSAIDs

Non-steroidal anti-inflammatory drugs (NSAIDs) represent the gentlest approach to reducing brain inflammation in PANDAS/PANS. These medications that many families already have in their medicine cabinets can sometimes provide surprising relief for neuropsychiatric symptoms.

Ibuprofen is the most commonly used NSAID in PANDAS/PANS treatment. The typical dose is 10-15 mg/kg three times daily with food, which often means 200-400mg three times daily for school-age children. Some specialists recommend higher doses, up to 20 mg/kg three times daily, but this requires careful monitoring for side effects.

The anti-inflammatory effects of NSAIDs go beyond simple pain relief. These medications reduce the production of inflammatory substances called prostaglandins and can cross the blood-brain barrier to reduce neuroinflammation directly. Some children show remarkable improvement in OCD, tics, and behavioral symptoms with NSAIDs alone.

Naproxen offers the advantage of twice-daily dosing, which can improve compliance in children who resist taking multiple medications. The typical dose is 5-10 mg/kg twice daily with food. The longer duration of action may provide more consistent anti-inflammatory effects throughout the day.

NSAIDs work best when used consistently rather than on an as-needed basis. Many parents make the mistake of giving ibuprofen only during symptom flares, but sustained anti-inflammatory treatment is usually necessary to see neuropsychiatric benefits.

The response to NSAIDs can be dramatic in some children and minimal in others. Those who respond well often show improvement within days to weeks of starting treatment. Children who don't respond to one NSAID may respond to another, so it's worth trying different options.

Safety considerations for extended NSAID use include monitoring for gastrointestinal upset, kidney function, and cardiovascular effects. Most children tolerate NSAIDs well for months of treatment, but regular check-ins with healthcare providers are important for catching any problems early.

Combining NSAIDs with gastric protection using proton pump inhibitors or H2 blockers may be necessary for children who develop stomach upset. Taking NSAIDs with food and ensuring adequate hydration also helps minimize gastrointestinal side effects.

Corticosteroids and Their Complex Role

Corticosteroids like prednisone represent the most powerful anti-inflammatory medications available for PANDAS/PANS treatment. These medications can provide dramatic improvement in children who haven't responded adequately to antibiotics or NSAIDs, but they come with significant side effects that require careful consideration.

The typical prednisone protocol for PANDAS/PANS involves high doses initially (1-2 mg/kg daily, often 20-60mg daily for children) followed by gradual tapering over several weeks. Some children respond to shorter courses of 1-2 weeks, while others need longer treatment periods.

The response to corticosteroids can be remarkable. Children with severe OCD who couldn't function normally may show substantial improvement within days of starting treatment. Tics often improve dramatically, and the explosive rage episodes that terrify families frequently resolve quickly.

However, **corticosteroids affect virtually every system in the body** and can cause significant side effects, especially with longer courses. Weight gain, mood changes, elevated blood sugar, and increased infection risk are common concerns. Children may develop "steroid rage" - irritability and emotional lability that can worsen behavioral problems.

Sleep disruption is almost universal with corticosteroid treatment. Children often have difficulty falling asleep and may wake frequently during the night. This sleep disruption can worsen PANDAS/PANS symptoms, creating a challenging situation for families.

Growth suppression can occur with extended corticosteroid use, making these medications particularly concerning for younger children. Most specialists limit corticosteroid courses to the shortest effective duration and monitor growth parameters carefully.

The decision to use corticosteroids often depends on symptom severity and response to other treatments. Children with mild symptoms usually try other approaches first, while those with severe, life-disrupting symptoms may need corticosteroids to achieve rapid stabilization.

Tapering corticosteroids requires careful planning because stopping too quickly can lead to symptom rebound that's worse than the original presentation. Most protocols involve gradual dose reductions over 2-4 weeks, with slower tapering if symptoms begin returning.

IVIG and Advanced Interventions

Intravenous immunoglobulin (IVIG) represents the most intensive immunomodulatory treatment for PANDAS/PANS. This treatment involves infusing antibodies pooled from thousands of donors, which can help reset the immune system and reduce autoimmune inflammation affecting the brain.

IVIG is typically reserved for children with severe symptoms who haven't responded adequately to less intensive treatments. The procedure requires hospitalization or infusion center treatment over 1-2 days, making it significantly more complex and expensive than oral medications.

The mechanism of IVIG in PANDAS/PANS isn't completely understood, but it likely works through multiple pathways. The infused antibodies may neutralize pathogenic antibodies attacking brain tissue, modulate immune cell function, and provide anti-inflammatory effects throughout the body.

Studies suggest that approximately 60-70% of children with PANDAS/PANS show significant improvement with IVIG treatment . The response often begins within days of treatment and may continue improving for weeks afterward. Some children experience complete symptom resolution that lasts for months or years.

IVIG protocols vary among treatment centers, but most use doses of 1-2 grams per kilogram of body weight given over 1-2 days. Some centers prefer single high-dose treatments, while others give divided doses. The optimal dosing and scheduling remain areas of ongoing research.

Side effects during IVIG infusion can include headaches, fever, chills, and allergic reactions. Most side effects are mild and resolve quickly, but serious reactions occasionally occur. Premedication with antihistamines and corticosteroids can reduce the risk of adverse reactions.

Access to IVIG remains challenging for many families due to cost and insurance coverage issues. The treatment can cost $20,000-$50,000 or more, and many insurance companies consider it experimental for PANDAS/PANS despite growing evidence of effectiveness.

Plasmapheresis and Cutting-Edge Options

Plasmapheresis (plasma exchange) involves removing the child's blood, separating out the plasma containing harmful antibodies, and returning the blood cells with replacement plasma or albumin. This procedure physically removes the autoimmune antibodies that may be attacking brain tissue.

Research suggests that plasmapheresis may be even more effective than IVIG for some children with PANDAS/PANS (Perlmutter et al., 1999). The procedure provides more rapid removal of pathogenic antibodies compared to the gradual immune modulation achieved with IVIG.

Plasmapheresis requires specialized medical centers and carries higher risks than IVIG. The procedure typically involves 5-7 treatments over 2-3 weeks, with each session lasting 2-4 hours. Children usually need central venous access, which requires surgical placement of a catheter.

The dramatic nature of plasmapheresis responses can be striking. Some children show substantial improvement after just 1-2 treatments, with continued progress over the full course. However, not all children respond, and some may need repeated courses.

Rituximab represents another advanced treatment option for severe, refractory PANDAS/PANS cases. This medication targets B cells that produce antibodies, potentially reducing the production of harmful autoimmune antibodies. However, rituximab suppresses immune function significantly and carries substantial risks.

Other experimental treatments under investigation include cyclophosphamide, mycophenolate mofetil, and various biologics used in autoimmune diseases. These treatments are typically reserved for the most severe cases that haven't responded to standard therapies.

Supplement-Based Immune Support

Omega-3 fatty acids provide natural anti-inflammatory effects that may benefit children with PANDAS/PANS. Fish oil supplements containing EPA and DHA can help reduce systemic inflammation and support brain health. Typical doses range from 1-3 grams daily of combined EPA and DHA.

Vitamin D deficiency is common in children with PANDAS/PANS and may contribute to immune dysfunction . Correcting vitamin D levels with supplementation can improve immune function and may reduce symptom severity. Most children need 1000-4000 IU daily, depending on baseline levels.

Curcumin, the active compound in turmeric, provides potent anti-inflammatory effects and may help reduce brain inflammation. However, curcumin has poor absorption when taken alone, so supplements containing piperine or other absorption enhancers are preferable.

N-acetylcysteine (NAC) has shown promise for reducing OCD symptoms and may have anti-inflammatory effects relevant to PANDAS/PANS. Typical doses range from 600-1800mg daily, usually divided into 2-3 doses. Some children show improvement in both OCD and tics with NAC supplementation.

Probiotics may help modulate immune function by supporting healthy gut bacteria populations. Multi-strain probiotics containing Lactobacillus and Bifidobacterium species are typically recommended. Some research suggests specific strains may be particularly beneficial for immune regulation.

Magnesium supplementation can help with tics, sleep problems, and anxiety that commonly occur in PANDAS/PANS. Magnesium glycinate or magnesium taurate are well-absorbed forms that are less likely to cause gastrointestinal upset than magnesium oxide.

Timing and Treatment Sequencing

The sequence of immunomodulatory treatments can significantly impact outcomes. Most specialists start with the gentlest approaches and escalate to more intensive treatments only when necessary. This approach minimizes side effects while allowing time to assess treatment responses.

A typical treatment sequence might begin with NSAIDs combined with antibiotics, progress to short corticosteroid courses if needed, and reserve IVIG or plasmapheresis for severe cases that don't respond to less intensive interventions.

Combination approaches often work better than single treatments. Many children benefit from combining antibiotics with anti-inflammatory medications, or using supplements to support more intensive medical treatments. The art lies in finding the right combination for each individual child.

Timing treatments around symptom flares can be particularly effective. Some families learn to recognize early signs of symptom worsening and initiate anti-inflammatory treatments quickly to prevent full flares from developing.

Maintenance therapy may be necessary for some children who experience symptom recurrence when treatments are discontinued. Low-dose anti-inflammatory medications or supplements may help maintain stability while minimizing side effects.

The goal is always to use the least intensive treatment that provides adequate symptom control. Many children can eventually discontinue immunomodulatory treatments once their immune systems stabilize, though this process may take months or years.

Real-World Treatment Journeys

Consider 10-year-old Jake, whose severe tics and OCD improved dramatically with a two-week course of prednisone. However, symptoms returned when the steroid was tapered. His doctor then added ibuprofen for maintenance anti-inflammatory effects, allowing successful steroid withdrawal while maintaining symptom control.

Thirteen-year-old Ashley didn't respond adequately to antibiotics alone but showed remarkable improvement when ibuprofen was added to her treatment regimen. The combination of azithromycin and ibuprofen controlled her symptoms for eight months before she could discontinue both medications.

Eight-year-old David required IVIG treatment after failing to respond to multiple combinations of antibiotics and anti-inflammatory medications. The IVIG provided dramatic improvement that lasted for over a year, with only mild symptoms recurring during subsequent infections.

Essential Treatment Principles:

- Start with gentler anti-inflammatory approaches before considering intensive interventions

- Combination treatments often work better than single agents

- Response timing varies - some children improve quickly while others need weeks to show benefits

- Side effect monitoring is crucial, especially with corticosteroids and advanced treatments

- Maintenance therapy may be necessary to prevent symptom recurrence

- Work with experienced providers who understand the complex treatment decisions involved

- Don't give up if initial treatments don't work - many children need multiple approaches to achieve stabilit

Chapter 6: Managing Neuropsychiatric Symptoms

The therapist's office felt foreign to 9-year-old Alex, who sat rigidly in the chair, afraid to touch anything because of contamination fears. His mother, Linda, had explained the situation multiple times: "He didn't have OCD before this started. This all began six weeks ago, completely out of the blue."

Dr. Sullivan nodded thoughtfully. She'd been treating children with anxiety and OCD for fifteen years, but PANDAS/PANS cases required a completely different approach. Traditional therapy techniques that worked beautifully for typical childhood OCD could actually backfire with these kids, sometimes making symptoms worse instead of better.

This is where many families get stuck. They find therapists who specialize in pediatric OCD or anxiety, expecting standard treatment approaches to work. But PANDAS/PANS creates a unique situation where the brain inflammation driving symptoms can make children less responsive to psychological interventions - at least initially.

CBT Adaptations for Inflamed Brains

Cognitive Behavioral Therapy (CBT) remains valuable for PANDAS/PANS, but it needs significant modifications to account for the medical nature of these conditions. Traditional CBT assumes that children can engage their rational thinking to challenge irrational thoughts, but brain inflammation can make this process much more difficult.

The timing of CBT matters enormously. Starting intensive therapy during acute symptom phases often frustrates both children and therapists because the neuroinflammation interferes with the cognitive flexibility needed for CBT techniques to work effectively.

Modified CBT for PANDAS/PANS focuses heavily on psychoeducation - helping children and families understand that their symptoms have a medical cause. This understanding alone can reduce the shame and self-blame that often accompany sudden-onset psychiatric symptoms.

Instead of immediately challenging obsessive thoughts, therapists working with PANDAS/PANS children often start by validating how frightening and confusing the symptoms must feel. "Your brain is fighting an infection right now, and that's making it send false alarm signals" can be more helpful than "Let's examine the evidence for this worry."

Flexibility becomes essential in therapy sessions. A child might have a great session one week and be completely unable to engage the next week due to symptom fluctuations. Therapists need to adjust their expectations and approaches based on current symptom levels rather than following rigid treatment protocols.

Family involvement takes on even greater importance in PANDAS/PANS cases. Parents need education about when to push their child to use coping skills versus when to accommodate symptoms temporarily while medical treatments take effect.

Gradual exposure principles still apply, but the pacing may need to be much slower than with typical OCD. Children with PANDAS/PANS may need weeks or months to make progress that typical OCD patients achieve in days or weeks.

ERP Therapy with Medical Considerations

Exposure and Response Prevention (ERP) therapy is considered the gold standard for OCD treatment, but it requires careful modification for children with PANDAS/PANS. The basic principle - gradually exposing children to their fears while preventing compulsive responses - remains valid, but the implementation needs adjustment.

Standard ERP protocols often move too quickly for children whose brains are fighting inflammation. What looks like treatment resistance may actually be a child's brain lacking the neurological capacity to inhibit compulsive responses due to ongoing autoimmune activity.

Starting ERP before medical treatment has begun often fails and can traumatize children who simply don't have the neurological resources to resist their compulsions. Many specialists recommend waiting until medical treatments have provided some symptom reduction before beginning intensive ERP.

The hierarchy of exposures may need frequent revision as symptoms fluctuate. A child might master touching doorknobs one week but become unable to do so the next week due to symptom flares. Therapists need to adapt rather than interpret this as treatment resistance.

Family accommodation - the ways families modify their behavior to reduce a child's distress - requires nuanced handling in PANDAS/PANS. While reducing accommodation is typically important in OCD treatment, some temporary accommodation may be necessary during acute symptom phases.

Parents need guidance about which accommodations to reduce gradually versus which ones to maintain temporarily. For example, helping a child with handwashing rituals might be accommodated during severe symptom phases while working to reduce checking behaviors that are less severe.

Response prevention needs to be graduated more carefully than in typical OCD treatment. Complete prevention of compulsions may be impossible during acute phases, so therapists often focus on reducing the frequency or intensity of rituals rather than eliminating them entirely initially.

Psychiatric Medications in PANDAS/PANS

Selective serotonin reuptake inhibitors (SSRIs) can be helpful for PANDAS/PANS symptoms, but they often work differently than in typical pediatric OCD. Some children respond well to SSRIs, while others experience increased agitation, mood swings, or behavioral activation that requires medication discontinuation.

The "start low and go slow" principle becomes even more important with PANDAS/PANS. Many children are more sensitive to psychiatric medications during acute phases, requiring lower starting doses and more gradual increases than typically recommended.

Sertraline and fluoxetine are most commonly used SSRIs for PANDAS/PANS, but response patterns can be unpredictable. Some children who don't respond to one SSRI may respond well to another, though medication trials need to be long enough to assess effectiveness - usually 8-12 weeks at therapeutic doses.

Tricyclic antidepressants like clomipramine may be effective for children who don't respond to SSRIs, though the side effect profile requires careful monitoring. Some children seem to respond better to medications that affect multiple neurotransmitter systems rather than just serotonin.

Stimulant medications for attention problems need careful consideration in PANDAS/PANS. These medications can worsen tics and increase agitation in some children, though others benefit from improved focus and reduced hyperactivity. Starting with very low doses and monitoring closely is essential.

Atypical antipsychotics like risperidone or aripiprazole may be helpful for severe behavioral symptoms, tics, or mood instability that don't respond to other approaches. However, these medications carry significant side effect risks and should generally be reserved for severe cases.

Mood stabilizers may be necessary for children who develop significant mood swings or rage episodes. Lamotrigine, lithium, or anticonvulsants like valproic acid have been used successfully in some PANDAS/PANS cases, though evidence is limited.

Managing Severe Behavioral Symptoms

Rage episodes in PANDAS/PANS can be terrifying for families and require specific management strategies that differ from typical behavioral interventions. These episodes often have a neurological component that makes standard behavioral techniques less effective.

During acute rage episodes, safety becomes the primary concern. Families need plans for protecting the child, siblings, and property during these episodes. Sometimes this means clearing the area of breakable objects or having safe spaces where the child can be alone until the episode passes.

De-escalation techniques need modification for PANDAS/PANS-related rage. Traditional approaches like reasoning or trying to redirect attention often backfire because the child's brain isn't capable of engaging these higher-level cognitive processes during acute episodes.

Simple, concrete interventions work better than complex behavioral strategies. Dimming lights, reducing noise, and providing physical comfort (if the child accepts it) can help more than trying to talk through the episode.

Preventing rage episodes often requires identifying and avoiding triggers when possible. Common triggers include being rushed, unexpected changes in routine, sensory overload, fatigue, and hunger. Families learn to modify their environment and expectations during symptomatic periods.

Some children benefit from having a "rage box" with safe objects they can throw or hit during episodes. Others respond well to heavy work activities like jumping on trampolines or pushing heavy objects that provide proprioceptive input.

Recovery after rage episodes needs attention too. Children often feel ashamed and confused about their behavior, requiring reassurance that the episode was caused by their medical condition, not character flaws. Processing these episodes when the child is calm can help reduce future intensity.

Crisis Intervention Strategies

Developing crisis plans before they're needed helps families respond effectively during severe symptom exacerbations. These plans should address safety concerns, medication adjustments, school accommodations, and when to seek emergency care.

Emergency department visits for PANDAS/PANS can be frustrating because most emergency physicians aren't familiar with these conditions. Bringing documentation about the child's diagnosis and current treatments can help emergency staff understand the medical nature of the crisis.

Psychiatric hospitalization occasionally becomes necessary for children with severe symptoms that pose safety risks. However, many psychiatric units aren't equipped to manage PANDAS/PANS appropriately, potentially leading to ineffective treatment or worsening of symptoms.

When hospitalization is necessary, families should advocate for medical evaluation alongside psychiatric treatment. Adjusting medications, starting anti-inflammatory treatments, or addressing infections may be more helpful than traditional psychiatric interventions alone.

Intensive outpatient programs may provide better options than hospitalization for many children. These programs can provide daily support while allowing children to remain at home and maintain some normal routines.

Therapy During Active Flares

The goals of therapy shift during active symptom flares from skill-building and symptom reduction to support and safety. Trying to push through intensive therapy during severe symptom phases often creates additional stress without meaningful progress.

Therapists need training in recognizing when children are in active flares versus stable periods. The same child who could engage in sophisticated CBT techniques last month might only be capable of basic coping strategies during a symptom exacerbation.

Family therapy becomes particularly important during flares because the entire family system gets disrupted. Parents need support, siblings need attention, and everyone needs help understanding that the current situation is temporary.

Maintaining some therapeutic contact during flares can be valuable, even if traditional therapy techniques aren't possible. Brief check-ins, crisis planning, or simply providing support can help families feel less isolated.

School-based interventions need coordination with medical treatment during flares. Therapists can help advocate for appropriate accommodations and educate school staff about the child's condition.

Success Stories from the Therapy Room

Consider 12-year-old Maya, whose contamination fears made traditional ERP impossible initially. Her therapist focused on medical education and family support while Maya received antibiotic treatment. After three months of medical treatment, Maya was able to engage in modified ERP that led to significant improvement.

Ten-year-old Connor's rage episodes were so severe that his family couldn't leave their house. His therapist worked with the family to identify early warning signs and develop safety plans. As medical treatments reduced the frequency of episodes, behavioral interventions became more effective.

Eleven-year-old Sophie couldn't tolerate SSRIs during her acute phase but responded well to them after three months of antibiotic and anti-inflammatory treatment. The combination of medical treatment followed by appropriate psychiatric medication and therapy led to complete symptom resolution.

Key Principles for Therapeutic Success:

- Timing matters - intensive therapy works best after medical treatment has begun

- Flexibility in approach is essential due to symptom fluctuations

- Family education and support are crucial components of treatment
- Crisis planning prevents emergency situations from becoming traumatic
- Standard therapy techniques need modification for inflamed brains
- Medication responses can be unpredictable and require careful monitoring
- Recovery is possible with appropriate combination of medical and psychological interventions
- Don't give up if initial approaches don't work - these children often need creative, individualized treatment plans

Chapter 7: Holistic Support - Nutrition and Lifestyle

Sandra watched her 11-year-old son Michael push his plate away for the third night in a row. "I can't eat this," he said, his voice tight with anxiety. "It doesn't feel safe." Six months ago, Michael would eat anything she put in front of him. Now, his food restrictions had narrowed to just five items, and even those had to be prepared in specific ways.

The irony wasn't lost on Sandra. Here she was, trying to implement an anti-inflammatory diet to help Michael's PANDAS symptoms, while he could barely tolerate any foods at all. **This scenario plays out in countless homes dealing with PANDAS/PANS - parents desperately wanting to support their child's healing through nutrition while battling the very food restrictions that the condition creates.**

But here's what Sandra didn't know yet: supporting a child's recovery from PANDAS/PANS goes far beyond just medical treatments. The foods they eat, how well they sleep, their stress levels, and even their exposure to environmental toxins can all influence the inflammatory processes driving their symptoms.

Anti-inflammatory Nutrition Protocols

Think of food as medicine during your child's recovery. Every meal represents an opportunity to either fuel inflammation or help calm it down. The standard American diet - heavy on processed foods, sugar, and omega-6 fatty acids - tends to promote inflammation throughout the body, including the brain.

The Mediterranean diet provides an excellent foundation for anti-inflammatory eating. This approach emphasizes fresh fruits and vegetables, whole grains, lean proteins (especially fish), nuts, seeds, and olive oil while limiting processed foods and refined sugars. Research shows that Mediterranean-style diets can significantly reduce inflammatory markers in both children and adults (Estruch et al., 2013).

Omega-3 fatty acids deserve special attention because they're among the most powerful anti-inflammatory nutrients available. Cold-water fish like salmon, mackerel, sardines, and tuna provide EPA and DHA - the specific omega-3s that cross the blood-brain barrier and help reduce neuroinflammation. Aim for at least two servings of fatty fish per week, or consider high-quality fish oil supplements if your child won't eat fish.

Colorful fruits and vegetables provide antioxidants and phytonutrients that fight inflammation. Blueberries, cherries, leafy greens, and brightly colored vegetables contain compounds that can help calm overactive immune responses. The deeper and more varied the colors on your child's plate, the better.

Turmeric and ginger stand out as particularly powerful anti-inflammatory spices. Turmeric contains curcumin, which has been shown to reduce brain inflammation and may help with OCD symptoms (Ng et al., 2017). Fresh ginger or ground ginger can be added to smoothies, soups, or teas to provide anti-inflammatory benefits that children often find palatable.

Green tea provides L-theanine, an amino acid that can help reduce anxiety and promote calmness without sedation. Many children find iced green tea more appealing than hot tea, and you can add a small amount of honey for sweetness if needed.

Probiotic-rich foods support gut health, which directly impacts immune function and inflammation. Plain yogurt with live cultures, kefir, sauerkraut, and other fermented foods can help restore healthy gut bacteria populations that may have been disrupted by antibiotic treatments.

Identifying and Eliminating Trigger Foods

Food sensitivities can worsen inflammation and PANDAS/PANS symptoms, even in children who never had food problems before.

The immune system dysfunction that drives these conditions can create new sensitivities to foods that were previously well-tolerated.

Common inflammatory foods include refined sugars, artificial food dyes, preservatives, and highly processed foods. Some children also react to gluten, dairy, soy, or specific food additives. The challenge lies in identifying which foods might be problematic for your specific child.

An elimination diet represents the gold standard for identifying food triggers. This process involves removing suspected foods for 2-4 weeks, then systematically reintroducing them one at a time while monitoring for symptom changes. It's time-consuming and requires careful planning, but it can provide invaluable information about your child's individual triggers.

Start with the most common inflammatory foods: sugar, artificial colors and flavors, preservatives, and highly processed items. Many families are amazed by how much better their children feel just by eliminating artificial food dyes and excessive sugar from their diets.

Keep a detailed food and symptom diary during any elimination process. Note what your child eats at each meal and snack, along with symptom levels throughout the day. Patterns often emerge after several weeks of consistent tracking that might not be obvious day-to-day.

Some children with PANDAS/PANS develop reactions to foods high in glutamates, including aged cheeses, processed meats, and foods containing MSG. Others seem sensitive to histamine-rich foods like aged or fermented items, citrus fruits, or chocolate.

Working with a nutritionist experienced in food sensitivities can make the elimination process more manageable and ensure your child maintains adequate nutrition while identifying triggers. Many families try to do this alone and end up with overly restrictive diets that create more problems than they solve.

Gut Health and the Microbiome Connection

The gut-brain axis represents a crucial pathway connecting digestive health with neurological and psychiatric symptoms. The trillions of bacteria living in your child's intestines communicate directly with the brain through multiple pathways, influencing mood, behavior, and immune function.

Children with PANDAS/PANS often have disrupted gut microbiomes due to antibiotic treatments, stress, and the inflammatory processes associated with their condition. This disruption can perpetuate symptoms and interfere with recovery even after the initial triggers have been addressed.

Restoring healthy gut bacteria requires more than just taking probiotic supplements, though these can be helpful. The gut microbiome responds to dietary choices, stress levels, sleep patterns, and antibiotic exposure. A holistic approach addresses all these factors simultaneously.

Prebiotic foods feed beneficial bacteria and may be just as important as probiotics themselves. Foods high in prebiotic fiber include garlic, onions, asparagus, bananas, oats, and flaxseeds. These foods provide the fuel that good bacteria need to thrive and multiply.

Bone broth provides nutrients that support gut lining integrity and can be particularly beneficial for children whose digestive systems have been stressed by illness or medications. Homemade bone broth simmered for 12-24 hours extracts beneficial compounds like collagen, glycine, and glutamine that support gut healing.

Fermented foods offer diverse strains of beneficial bacteria that supplements may not provide. Start with small amounts of fermented vegetables, kefir, or plain yogurt and gradually increase portions as your child's digestive system adapts.

Avoiding unnecessary antibiotics helps preserve gut microbiome diversity, though this needs to be balanced against the therapeutic need for antibiotics in PANDAS/PANS treatment. When antibiotics are necessary, concurrent probiotic supplementation can help minimize microbiome disruption.

Sleep Optimization Strategies

Sleep problems affect nearly every child with PANDAS/PANS, and poor sleep can significantly worsen neuropsychiatric symptoms. The inflammatory processes driving these conditions can disrupt normal sleep architecture, while the anxiety and compulsions make it difficult for children to relax at bedtime.

Creating a consistent bedtime routine becomes even more important for children with PANDAS/PANS than for typical children. The routine should begin 1-2 hours before desired sleep time and include calming activities that help transition the nervous system from alertness to relaxation.

Environmental modifications can significantly impact sleep quality. The bedroom should be cool (around 65-68°F), dark, and quiet. Consider blackout curtains, white noise machines, or earplugs if needed. Remove electronic devices at least one hour before bedtime, as blue light exposure can interfere with melatonin production.

Many children with PANDAS/PANS benefit from weighted blankets, which provide deep pressure stimulation that can help calm the nervous system. The weight should be approximately 10% of the child's body weight plus 1-2 pounds for optimal effectiveness.

Melatonin supplementation can be helpful for children with persistent sleep problems, but timing and dosage matter enormously. Low doses (0.5-3mg) given 30-60 minutes before desired sleep time work better than higher doses given closer to bedtime. Some children respond better to extended-release formulations.

Magnesium supplementation before bedtime can help with both sleep and muscle relaxation. Magnesium glycinate or magnesium taurate are well-absorbed forms that are less likely to cause digestive upset than magnesium oxide.

Address anxiety and compulsions that interfere with sleep through a combination of medical treatment and behavioral strategies. Some children need modified bedtime routines that accommodate their compulsions temporarily while working toward reducing them over time.

Stress Reduction for the Whole Family

PANDAS/PANS creates stress for everyone in the family, and that stress can perpetuate the child's symptoms through multiple pathways. Stress hormones like cortisol can worsen inflammation and interfere with immune function, creating a cycle where family stress worsens the child's condition, which increases family stress further.

Teaching simple stress reduction techniques that the whole family can use together creates shared coping strategies and reduces the feeling that the affected child is "different" or "broken." Deep breathing exercises, progressive muscle relaxation, and mindfulness activities can benefit everyone.

Yoga adapted for children can provide both physical exercise and stress reduction. Many communities offer family yoga classes, or you can follow online videos designed for children. The combination of movement, breathing, and mindfulness can be particularly beneficial for kids with anxiety and OCD symptoms.

Creating calm spaces in your home gives family members places to retreat when feeling overwhelmed. This might be a cozy reading corner, a meditation space, or just a quiet bedroom where people can decompress without interruption.

Regular family meetings help everyone feel heard and involved in problem-solving. These don't need to be formal or lengthy - even 10-15 minutes weekly can help family members share concerns and brainstorm solutions together.

Limiting exposure to stressful news, social media, or other anxiety-provoking content helps protect the whole family's mental health. Children with PANDAS/PANS are often particularly sensitive to external stressors that wouldn't have bothered them before their illness.

Professional stress management support may be beneficial for parents who are struggling to cope. Stress management counseling, support groups, or individual therapy can help parents develop better coping strategies, which ultimately benefits the entire family.

Exercise and Movement Therapy

Physical activity provides multiple benefits for children with PANDAS/PANS, including stress reduction, improved sleep, enhanced mood, and better overall health. However, the type and intensity of exercise may need modification based on your child's current symptom levels and physical capabilities.

Gentle, rhythmic activities often work better than high-intensity or competitive sports during symptomatic periods. Walking, swimming, cycling, or dancing can provide exercise benefits without overwhelming an already stressed nervous system.

Martial arts programs designed for children can be particularly beneficial because they combine physical activity with mental discipline and stress reduction techniques. Many children with PANDAS/PANS respond well to the structure and mindfulness components of martial arts training.

Team sports may be challenging during acute symptom phases due to social difficulties, concentration problems, or tics that make children self-conscious. Individual or small group activities often feel more manageable and less stressful.

Sensory integration activities can help children whose PANDAS/PANS symptoms include sensory processing difficulties. Occupational therapists can recommend specific exercises that provide the sensory input children need to feel more regulated and calm.

Heavy work activities - like carrying groceries, rearranging furniture, or doing push-ups against walls - provide proprioceptive input that many children find calming. These activities can be incorporated into daily routines without requiring formal exercise programs.

Monitor your child's response to different types of physical activity and adjust accordingly. Some children feel better with daily gentle exercise, while others do better with more intense activity less frequently. Let your child's response guide your decisions.

Environmental Toxin Considerations

Environmental toxins can worsen inflammation and interfere with immune function, potentially exacerbating PANDAS/PANS symptoms. While you can't control every environmental exposure, making simple changes can reduce your child's toxic burden.

Indoor air quality affects children significantly because they spend most of their time indoors. Common indoor pollutants include cleaning products, air fresheners, candles, and off-gassing from furniture or carpets. Switching to natural cleaning products and improving ventilation can help reduce exposure.

Mold exposure can be particularly problematic for children with immune dysfunction. If your home has water damage, persistent humidity problems, or visible mold growth, professional remediation may be necessary. Some children are extremely sensitive to mold and show significant symptom improvement after mold exposure is eliminated.

Personal care products - shampoos, soaps, lotions, and toothpastes - often contain chemicals that can disrupt hormone function or increase inflammatory load. Switching to more natural alternatives reduces daily chemical exposure without major lifestyle changes.

Water quality matters because children drink and bathe in water daily. If your tap water contains chlorine, fluoride, or other chemicals that concern you, consider water filtration systems. Some families notice improvements in their child's symptoms after switching to filtered water.

Pesticide residues on conventionally grown fruits and vegetables can add to toxic burden. The Environmental Working Group publishes annual lists of the "Dirty Dozen" and "Clean Fifteen" - foods with the highest and lowest pesticide residues. Prioritizing organic versions of high-residue foods can reduce exposure while managing costs.

Electromagnetic field (EMF) exposure from WiFi, cell phones, and other electronic devices concerns some families, though research on health effects remains mixed. Simple precautions like keeping devices out of bedrooms and limiting screen time may provide benefits beyond just EMF reduction.

Real-World Implementation Stories

Consider the Johnson family, whose 9-year-old daughter Sarah had severe food restrictions during her PANDAS episode. Instead of fighting the restrictions, they worked with Sarah's limited acceptable foods to create anti-inflammatory versions. They found organic versions of her safe foods, eliminated artificial colors and preservatives, and gradually expanded her diet as her symptoms improved with medical treatment.

The Martinez family discovered that their 12-year-old son Carlos was sensitive to artificial food dyes after noticing his tics worsened dramatically after birthday parties or school events with lots of processed foods. Eliminating artificial colors led to a 50% reduction in tic frequency within two weeks.

Ten-year-old Emma's family implemented a comprehensive approach that included dietary changes, sleep optimization, and stress reduction techniques. While no single intervention was dramatic, the combination of approaches helped Emma maintain stability and reduced the frequency of symptom flares.

Your Holistic Support Game Plan:

- Start with one area - nutrition, sleep, or stress reduction - rather than trying to change everything at once

- Track changes and symptoms to identify what helps your specific child

- Include the whole family in lifestyle changes to reduce the feeling that the affected child is "different"

- Work with professionals when needed, particularly for nutrition and exercise modifications

- Focus on reducing inflammation through multiple pathways simultaneously

- Be patient - lifestyle changes often take weeks or months to show full benefits

- Adapt approaches based on your child's current symptom levels and capabilities

- Don't let perfect be the enemy of good - small improvements add up over time

Chapter 8: Managing Flares and Setbacks

The text came at 11 PM on a Thursday: "Mom, I can't stop washing my hands. They're bleeding but I can't stop." Sixteen-year-old Jessica had been doing well for six months after her initial PANDAS episode. Her OCD symptoms had resolved, she was back to her normal social activities, and the family had started to believe the nightmare was behind them.

But here they were again. Jessica's father had developed strep throat three days earlier, and despite everyone's careful precautions, Jessica's symptoms had returned with a vengeance. **This scenario - the dreaded flare or setback - is one of the most challenging aspects of PANDAS/PANS for families to navigate.**

The emotional roller coaster is brutal. Just when you think you've gotten your child back, the symptoms return, often feeling worse than before because you've experienced what "normal" looks like again. The fear, the questions, the desperate scrambling to figure out what went wrong - it all comes flooding back.

Recognizing Early Signs of Flares

Learning to spot the subtle warning signs of an approaching flare can make the difference between a minor setback and a full-blown crisis. Many children show predictable patterns before major symptom exacerbations, but these early signs are often easy to miss if you're not watching for them.

Sleep changes frequently signal the beginning of a flare before other symptoms become obvious. Your child might start having trouble falling asleep, wake up more frequently during the night, or seem less rested despite getting adequate sleep. Some children begin having nightmares or night terrors that hadn't occurred in months.

Increased anxiety often appears days or weeks before obsessive-compulsive symptoms worsen. Your child might seem more clingy, ask for extra reassurance about routine activities, or avoid situations they had been handling well. This anxiety can be subtle initially - just a sense that they seem "off" or more fragile than usual.

Mild tics or repetitive behaviors may reappear before full-blown compulsions return. A child might start clearing their throat occasionally, blinking more frequently, or showing minor checking behaviors that had previously resolved completely.

Academic or social functioning may decline before dramatic symptoms appear. Teachers might notice decreased concentration, increased distractibility, or changes in handwriting quality. Friends or family members may comment that your child seems different or not quite themselves.

Physical symptoms can also herald approaching flares. Some children develop headaches, stomach aches, increased urination frequency, or changes in appetite before neuropsychiatric symptoms worsen. These physical changes may reflect early immune activation or stress responses.

Regression in previously mastered skills can be an early warning sign. A child might start having difficulty with tasks they had relearned during recovery, show increased dependency on parents for routine activities, or display emotional responses more typical of younger children.

Emergency Action Plans for Families

Having a written action plan before flares occur helps families respond quickly and effectively when symptoms worsen. This plan should outline specific steps to take at different levels of symptom severity, contact information for healthcare providers, and strategies for managing crisis situations.

The action plan should include criteria for recognizing mild, moderate, and severe symptom exacerbations. Mild flares might trigger increased monitoring and basic interventions, while severe flares require immediate medical attention and comprehensive safety planning.

Contact information should be readily available for all members of your child's treatment team, including primary care physicians, PANDAS/PANS specialists, mental health professionals, and emergency services. Include after-hours contact numbers and instructions for reaching providers outside normal business hours.

Medication protocols for flare management should be clearly outlined and easily accessible. This includes instructions for increasing existing medications, starting emergency medications if prescribed, and when to contact providers for dosage adjustments or new prescriptions.

Safety planning becomes crucial during severe flares when children may have suicidal thoughts, engage in self-harm behaviors, or become aggressive toward others. The plan should outline how to keep the child safe, when to remove dangerous objects from the environment, and when to seek emergency psychiatric evaluation.

Communication strategies help ensure all family members understand their roles during flares. This includes how to talk to siblings about what's happening, when to notify schools about symptom changes, and how to coordinate care among multiple providers.

Environmental modifications that help during flares should be documented so they can be implemented quickly. This might include reducing sensory stimulation, eliminating unnecessary demands or expectations, and creating calm spaces where the child can retreat when overwhelmed.

Treatment Intensification Strategies

Escalating treatment quickly during flares can prevent minor setbacks from becoming major crises. The specific intensification strategies depend on your child's baseline treatments and the severity of symptom recurrence.

Antibiotic treatment often needs to be started or intensified if flares are triggered by new infections. Having emergency prescriptions available or clear protocols for obtaining antibiotics quickly can prevent delays that allow symptoms to worsen.

Anti-inflammatory medications may need to be increased or added during flares. NSAIDs can often be started immediately while waiting for medical appointments, and some families have emergency prescriptions for corticosteroids to use during severe flares.

Existing psychiatric medications might need dosage adjustments or temporary additions during flares. Some children benefit from short-term increases in SSRI doses, while others need temporary anti-anxiety medications or sleep aids to manage acute symptoms.

Intensive therapy support may be necessary during flares, even if your child was doing well without regular therapy. Emergency therapy sessions can provide crisis intervention, family support, and modified coping strategies appropriate for current symptom levels.

Some children benefit from temporary return to more intensive medical monitoring during flares. This might include more frequent provider visits, laboratory monitoring, or coordination between multiple specialists to optimize treatment quickly.

IVIG or other immunomodulatory treatments might be considered for severe flares that don't respond to less intensive interventions. These treatments typically require pre-authorization and specialized medical centers, so planning ahead is essential.

Preventing Secondary Infections

Infection prevention becomes even more crucial after a child has experienced PANDAS/PANS because each new infection carries the risk of triggering another flare. This doesn't mean living in a bubble, but it does require thoughtful precautions and aggressive treatment of any infections that do occur.

Hand hygiene represents the most effective single intervention for preventing infections. Teaching proper handwashing techniques and ensuring children wash hands frequently, especially during high-risk periods like flu season, can significantly reduce infection risk.

Family member screening and treatment may be necessary to eliminate ongoing exposure sources. If family members develop strep throat or other infections, they should be tested and treated promptly to prevent transmission to the vulnerable child.

Prophylactic antibiotics during high-risk periods can prevent infections in some children. This approach is similar to rheumatic fever prevention protocols and may be particularly beneficial during flu season or when there are known strep outbreaks in schools or communities.

Environmental precautions during high-risk periods might include avoiding crowded places, limiting playdates during illness outbreaks, and keeping children home from school when they're feeling run-down or showing early signs of illness.

Immune system support through adequate sleep, good nutrition, stress reduction, and appropriate supplementation may help children resist infections. While these measures aren't guaranteed to prevent all illnesses, they can improve overall resilience.

Aggressive treatment of any new infections helps minimize the risk of triggering flares. Even minor respiratory infections should be evaluated promptly and treated aggressively with antibiotics if bacterial infection is suspected.

Emotional Support During Difficult Periods

Flares are traumatic for both children and families, often triggering feelings of hopelessness, anger, and fear that recovery might not be possible. Providing emotional support during these difficult periods is just as important as medical management.

Children often feel guilty and ashamed when symptoms return, particularly if they had been doing well for extended periods. They may worry that they caused the flare somehow or fear that their progress was all fake. Reassurance about the medical nature of their condition and the temporary nature of flares is essential.

Maintaining hope while acknowledging the reality of current difficulties requires delicate balance. Children need to understand that flares don't erase previous progress and that recovery is still possible, even if it takes longer than originally hoped.

Family members need support too, as watching a child suffer through repeated episodes can be emotionally exhausting. Parents may need reminders that setbacks don't mean they're failing their child or that previous treatment decisions were wrong.

Professional counseling during flares can provide crisis intervention and help families develop coping strategies for managing acute symptoms. Even children who don't normally need therapy may benefit from support during severe symptom exacerbations.

Sibling support becomes particularly important during flares because the entire family focus shifts back to the affected child's needs. Siblings may feel forgotten, angry, or scared about their brother or sister's condition returning.

Support groups - either in-person or online - can provide connections with other families who understand the unique challenges of PANDAS/PANS flares. Hearing from others who have navigated similar setbacks can provide hope and practical advice.

Learning from Setbacks Through Pattern Recognition

Every flare provides information that can help prevent or minimize future episodes. Systematic analysis of what preceded each setback can reveal patterns that might not be obvious during the crisis itself.

Keep detailed records of potential triggers, including infections, stressors, environmental changes, medication adjustments, or other factors that occurred before symptom worsening. Patterns often emerge after tracking several episodes.

Timing patterns can be particularly revealing. Some children experience flares seasonally, during specific times of the school year, or in relation to family stressors. Recognizing these patterns allows families to implement preventive measures during high-risk periods.

Treatment response patterns help guide future management decisions. Children who respond quickly to specific interventions during one flare are likely to benefit from similar approaches in future episodes.

Environmental factors that preceded flares should be examined carefully. Changes in housing, school, diet, or daily routines sometimes trigger symptom exacerbations in ways that aren't immediately obvious.

Stress levels and family functioning before flares can provide insights into triggers that are within the family's control. Major life changes, family conflicts, or academic pressures might contribute to vulnerability even if they don't directly cause flares.

Medical factors including medication changes, dose adjustments, or timing of treatments relative to flare onset can inform future treatment decisions. Some children are particularly sensitive to medication changes and need more gradual adjustments.

Success Stories from the Setback Trenches

The Williams family learned to recognize that their daughter Emma always developed minor sleep problems about a week before major flares. Once they identified this pattern, they implemented intensive sleep support and preventive anti-inflammatory treatment at the first sign of sleep disruption, significantly reducing both the frequency and severity of subsequent flares.

Twelve-year-old Alex's family discovered that his flares almost always occurred within two weeks of school starting each fall. They began implementing preventive strategies in August - including sleep schedule adjustments, stress reduction activities, and prophylactic anti-inflammatory treatment - which prevented major flares for two consecutive school years.

The Thompson family noticed that their son's flares were often preceded by family stress or conflict. They learned to recognize when household tension was building and implemented family stress reduction strategies, including regular family meetings and individual stress management techniques, which helped reduce both family stress and flare frequency.

Your Flare Management Toolkit:

- Develop written action plans before flares occur, not during crisis situations

- Learn your child's unique early warning signs and trust your parental instincts

- Have emergency medications and treatment protocols readily available

- Maintain relationships with experienced healthcare providers who understand PANDAS/PANS

- Track patterns systematically to identify triggers and effective interventions

- Focus on family emotional support as much as medical management

- Don't lose hope - flares are typically temporary setbacks, not permanent reversals

- Use each episode as a learning opportunity to improve future prevention and management

- Build support networks before you need them - crisis situations aren't ideal times to find help

Chapter 9: Educational Advocacy and School Support

The meeting room felt tense as Sarah sat across from five school personnel discussing her 10-year-old son David's educational needs. "He's been fine for months," the principal said, reviewing David's file. "His grades are good, he's not disruptive. I'm not sure why he needs special accommodations."

Sarah took a deep breath, trying to stay calm. How could she explain that David's "good" performance was costing him everything? That he was using every ounce of energy to appear normal at school, then coming home completely exhausted and melting down for hours? That his handwriting, which used to be neat, now took twice as long and caused him physical pain?

This scenario plays out in schools across the country every day. PANDAS/PANS creates educational challenges that don't fit neatly into traditional categories, leaving families struggling to advocate for children whose needs are invisible to most educators.

Understanding Your Child's Educational Rights

Every child with PANDAS/PANS has legal rights to appropriate educational support, even when their symptoms aren't obvious or don't fit traditional disability categories. These rights are protected under federal laws including the Individuals with Disabilities Education Act (IDEA) and Section 504 of the Rehabilitation Act.

The key principle underlying these laws is that children deserve access to free, appropriate public education regardless of their disabilities or medical conditions. This doesn't mean every child needs the same services, but rather that each child should receive the support necessary to benefit from their education.

IDEA provides the most comprehensive protections for children whose conditions significantly impact their educational performance. To qualify for IDEA services, children must have one of thirteen specific disability categories and demonstrate that their condition adversely affects educational performance.

Section 504 offers broader protections for children with any physical or mental impairment that substantially limits major life activities. The criteria for 504 eligibility are less stringent than IDEA, making this often the more accessible option for children with PANDAS/PANS.

Both laws require schools to provide appropriate accommodations and modifications at no cost to families. Schools cannot legally refuse to provide necessary services due to cost concerns or lack of familiarity with specific conditions.

The evaluation process represents your first step in accessing formal educational support. Schools are required to evaluate any child suspected of having a disability that affects their educational performance, and parents have the right to request these evaluations.

Documentation from medical providers strengthens your case for educational support but isn't always necessary for accessing services. Schools must consider all relevant information, including parent observations, teacher reports, and educational assessments.

504 Plans vs. IEPs for PANDAS/PANS

504 Plans typically provide the most appropriate framework for supporting children with PANDAS/PANS in school settings. These plans focus on removing barriers and providing accommodations that allow children to access the general education curriculum alongside their peers.

504 Plans are easier to implement and modify than Individualized Education Programs (IEPs), making them well-suited for conditions like PANDAS/PANS where symptoms fluctuate over time. Changes to 504 Plans can often be made quickly through team meetings rather than formal IEP processes.

IEPs may be necessary for children with more severe or persistent symptoms that require specialized instruction or related services like occupational therapy, speech therapy, or counseling. IEPs provide more comprehensive protections but also involve more complex processes.

The decision between 504 Plans and IEPs depends primarily on whether your child needs accommodations (504 Plan) or specialized instruction (IEP). Most children with PANDAS/PANS need accommodations to access existing curriculum rather than modified curriculum content.

504 Plans can be implemented more quickly than IEPs, which is important for children whose symptoms appear suddenly or change rapidly. The timeline for developing 504 Plans is more flexible than the strict timelines required for IEP development.

Both plans should be reviewed and updated regularly, but 504 Plans allow for more informal modifications as your child's needs change. This flexibility is particularly valuable for conditions like PANDAS/PANS where symptoms may improve dramatically or worsen unexpectedly.

Transition planning becomes important as children move between grade levels or schools. Both 504 Plans and IEPs should include provisions for sharing information with new teachers and ensuring continuity of services across transitions.

Essential Accommodations for Different Symptoms

Handwriting difficulties are among the most common educational impacts of PANDAS/PANS, often requiring multiple accommodations to address. These may include extended time for written assignments, permission to use computers or tablets for longer writing tasks, and reduced writing requirements when content mastery can be demonstrated other ways.

Fine motor problems affecting handwriting may also impact other school activities like art projects, science labs, or physical education. Occupational therapy evaluation can help identify specific areas of need and recommend appropriate accommodations.

Attention and concentration problems require accommodations that minimize distractions and provide structure for maintaining focus. These might include preferential seating away from high-traffic areas, frequent breaks during lengthy activities, and permission to use fidget tools or stress balls.

Test accommodations for attention difficulties may include extended time, separate testing environments, or breaks during long exams. Some children benefit from having tests read aloud or being allowed to give oral responses instead of written ones.

Anxiety-related accommodations help children manage school-specific fears and worries that may have developed during their PANDAS/PANS episode. These could include a designated safe person or place in the school, permission to leave class if anxiety becomes overwhelming, and advance notice of schedule changes or unexpected events.

Bathroom and water fountain accommodations may be necessary for children with contamination fears or compulsive behaviors. Some children need permission to use private bathrooms or bring their own water bottles to avoid triggers.

Social accommodations help children navigate peer interactions that may have become difficult during their illness. These might include structured social opportunities, lunch bunch groups with school counselors, or modified expectations for group work and presentations.

Communicating with Teachers and Administrators

Education is your most powerful tool for building understanding and support among school personnel. Most educators want to help children succeed but may lack knowledge about PANDAS/PANS and how it affects learning and behavior.

Provide written information about PANDAS/PANS, including reputable websites, research articles, and explanations from your child's medical providers. Focus on information that explains how the condition affects educational performance rather than detailed medical explanations.

Share specific examples of how symptoms impact your child's school experience. Instead of saying "he has anxiety," explain "he may need extra time to transition between activities because unexpected changes in routine can trigger panic attacks."

Regular communication helps build relationships and allows for quick problem-solving when issues arise. Many schools appreciate brief weekly emails updating them on your child's current symptom levels and any concerns you're observing at home.

Positive communication strengthens relationships and makes school personnel more willing to work collaboratively. Acknowledge efforts school staff make to support your child and express appreciation for their flexibility and understanding.

Training opportunities for school personnel can improve understanding and support for all students with PANDAS/PANS in the district. Offer to share resources or connect schools with experts who can provide professional development training.

Documentation of all communications protects both families and schools by creating clear records of discussions, agreements, and concerns. Follow up important conversations with emails summarizing what was discussed and agreed upon.

Handling School Refusal and Attendance Issues

School refusal - the inability or unwillingness to attend school due to anxiety, fear, or other emotional distress - affects many children with PANDAS/PANS and requires careful, coordinated intervention from both families and schools.

Traditional disciplinary approaches to attendance problems are inappropriate and counterproductive for children with medical conditions causing school avoidance. These children aren't choosing to miss school; they're experiencing genuine distress that makes attendance feel impossible.

Gradual reintegration plans often work better than forcing immediate return to full-time attendance. These plans might start with attending for one period per day and gradually increasing time at school as the child's comfort level improves.

Identifying specific triggers for school avoidance helps develop targeted interventions. Some children fear contamination in school bathrooms, others worry about having tics in front of classmates, and still others become overwhelmed by noise levels or schedule changes.

Modified schedules may be necessary temporarily while children are recovering from acute symptoms. This might include late start times, early dismissal, or attending only specific classes where the child feels most comfortable.

Home instruction services provide educational continuity when children cannot attend school due to medical conditions. These services are legally required for children whose medical conditions prevent school attendance, though accessing them may require medical documentation.

Mental health support at school can help address the anxiety and fear underlying school refusal. School counselors, social workers, or psychologists can provide crisis intervention and ongoing support to help children feel safer and more comfortable at school.

Academic Modifications During Treatment

Academic expectations may need temporary modification while children are receiving treatment for PANDAS/PANS. This doesn't mean lowering standards permanently, but rather providing flexibility during periods when symptoms interfere with learning.

Extended deadlines for assignments help accommodate the fatigue and concentration difficulties many children experience during treatment. Some children work much more slowly than usual due to compulsions, perfectionism, or difficulty focusing.

Modified homework expectations recognize that children may have limited energy for academics while dealing with symptoms and medical treatments. Reducing homework quantity while maintaining quality expectations can help maintain learning without overwhelming stressed children.

Testing modifications may include extended time, alternative testing formats, or rescheduling exams during symptom flares. Some children need oral testing instead of written exams, while others benefit from taking tests in small segments over multiple days.

Grade protection provisions prevent children from being penalized academically for symptoms beyond their control. This might include allowing incomplete grades that can be completed when symptoms improve, rather than failing grades that damage GPAs permanently.

Project modifications help children participate in longer-term assignments despite symptom fluctuations. Breaking large projects into smaller segments with interim deadlines can make them more manageable for children with attention or perfectionism issues.

Communication with teachers about current symptom levels helps them adjust expectations appropriately. Some children have good days and bad days that may not be predictable, requiring ongoing flexibility from educators.

Building a Supportive School Team

Identifying key allies within the school system helps ensure your child has support across multiple settings and situations. These allies might include teachers, counselors, administrators, nurses, or support staff who understand your child's needs.

The school nurse often serves as a crucial team member because they understand medical conditions and can provide health-related accommodations. Building a strong relationship with the nurse helps ensure appropriate response to medical needs during school hours.

Regular team meetings keep everyone informed about your child's progress and allow for quick adjustments to supports and accommodations. These meetings don't need to be formal IEP or 504 meetings - informal check-ins can be just as valuable.

Training opportunities help expand your support network by educating additional school personnel about PANDAS/PANS. Consider providing information to substitute teachers, specialists, and support staff who interact with your child.

Student advocacy programs can help older children learn to communicate their own needs and self-advocate for appropriate accommodations. Teaching children to explain their condition and request help builds skills they'll need throughout their lives.

Peer support and education may be appropriate for some children, particularly those whose symptoms are obvious to classmates. Age-appropriate explanations can reduce teasing and build understanding among peers.

Crisis planning with school teams ensures everyone knows how to respond if your child experiences severe symptoms at school. This includes procedures for contacting parents, providing emotional support, and ensuring safety during difficult episodes.

Real-World School Success Stories

Consider 8-year-old Maria, whose severe handwriting difficulties were impacting all subjects. Her school team worked together to provide a tablet for longer writing assignments while continuing to practice handwriting skills in shorter sessions. Within three months, Maria's academic performance improved dramatically, and her confidence returned.

Eleven-year-old Jason's contamination fears made school bathrooms impossible to use, leading to medical problems and school avoidance.

His school installed a motion-sensor soap dispenser and provided antibacterial wipes in a designated bathroom, allowing Jason to return to normal attendance.

Fourteen-year-old Ashley experienced severe anxiety about group presentations due to her tics. Her English teacher developed alternative assessment methods that allowed Ashley to demonstrate her knowledge through individual conferences and written reports instead of oral presentations.

Your School Advocacy Success Plan:

- Learn your legal rights and your child's entitlements under federal disability laws

- Document everything - symptoms, impacts on learning, communications with school

- Educate school personnel about PANDAS/PANS and its educational impacts

- Build positive relationships with key school team members

- Focus on specific accommodations tied to identified needs rather than general requests

- Stay flexible as your child's needs change with symptom fluctuations

- Celebrate successes and acknowledge school efforts to support your child

- Don't give up if initial efforts aren't successful - persistence often pays off

- Connect with other families for support and shared advocacy efforts

Chapter 10: Family Life and Emotional Support

The sound of 8-year-old Tyler screaming echoed through the house for the third time that week. His 12-year-old sister Megan slammed her bedroom door and turned up her music, while their parents exchanged weary glances across the kitchen table. "When is this going to end?" Megan had asked the night before. "When do I get to have a normal family again?"

PANDAS/PANS doesn't just affect the diagnosed child - it reshapes entire family systems in ways that can be both devastating and, ultimately, transformative. The condition demands so much attention and energy that other family members often feel invisible, forgotten, or resentful. Yet families who learn to navigate these challenges together often emerge stronger and more connected than before.

The statistics are sobering: studies show that families dealing with chronic childhood illness have divorce rates 10-15% higher than the general population, and siblings of children with medical conditions are at increased risk for emotional and behavioral problems (Raina et al., 2005). But these outcomes aren't inevitable. With intentional effort and appropriate support, families can not only survive but thrive through the PANDAS/PANS journey.

Protecting Sibling Relationships

Siblings of children with PANDAS/PANS face unique challenges that parents, overwhelmed by medical crises and daily management issues, often don't recognize. These children watch their brother or sister receive constant attention while their own needs take a backseat to medical appointments, therapy sessions, and symptom management.

The confusion siblings experience can be particularly intense because PANDAS/PANS symptoms are so dramatic and seemingly behavioral. Unlike clearly medical conditions like diabetes or cancer,

PANDAS/PANS can look like willful misbehavior to children who don't understand the underlying medical process.

Age-appropriate education helps siblings understand what's happening to their brother or sister and why family life has changed so dramatically. Younger children need simple explanations: "Jake's brain is sick right now, like when you have a fever, but the sick part makes him worried and scared instead of hot." Older children can understand more complex explanations about immune systems and brain inflammation.

Jealousy and resentment are normal responses that shouldn't be dismissed or minimized. Siblings often feel guilty about these feelings, which can compound their distress. Acknowledging that it's hard to watch a brother or sister get so much attention validates their experience while opening conversations about managing difficult emotions.

Individual attention for siblings becomes even more crucial during PANDAS/PANS episodes. This might mean one parent staying home with the affected child while the other attends a sibling's soccer game, or arranging special one-on-one time when the affected child is stable.

Creating separate spaces and activities helps siblings maintain their own identity and interests despite family disruption. Some siblings benefit from staying with extended family or friends during particularly difficult periods, giving them respite from the constant stress at home.

Sibling support groups - either in person or online - connect children with others who understand their unique experience. Many hospitals and mental health centers offer groups specifically for siblings of children with chronic medical conditions.

Managing Family Stress and Trauma

Living with PANDAS/PANS is traumatic for everyone in the family, though this trauma often goes unrecognized because the focus remains on the affected child's immediate needs. Parents may develop symptoms of post-traumatic stress disorder, including hypervigilance, sleep problems, and intrusive thoughts about their child's condition.

The unpredictability of PANDAS/PANS creates chronic stress that can be more difficult to manage than acute crises. Never knowing when symptoms might flare or how severe they might become keeps families in a constant state of alertness that's emotionally and physically exhausting.

Family therapy can provide crucial support during both acute phases and recovery periods. Therapists experienced in medical family therapy understand how chronic illness affects family dynamics and can help families develop healthier communication patterns and coping strategies.

Secondary trauma affects family members who witness the affected child's distress repeatedly. Parents often develop their own anxiety disorders, depression, or other mental health conditions that require professional treatment. Recognizing and addressing these secondary effects is essential for family stability.

Trauma-informed approaches help families understand how their responses to their child's condition might be normal reactions to abnormal circumstances. Symptoms like hypervigilance, difficulty concentrating, or emotional numbness may be trauma responses rather than character flaws.

Building resilience requires intentional effort to maintain family strengths and positive connections even during difficult periods. This might include family game nights during stable periods, maintaining traditions when possible, or creating new rituals that accommodate current limitations.

Professional support for parents may include individual therapy, couples counseling, or medication management for anxiety or depression. Taking care of parental mental health isn't selfish - it's essential for maintaining the family's ability to support the affected child.

Finding and Building Support Networks

Isolation is one of the most damaging aspects of dealing with PANDAS/PANS because the condition is so misunderstood and many families feel like they can't relate to others' experiences. Building connections with understanding people becomes essential for emotional survival.

Online support groups provide 24/7 access to others who understand the unique challenges of PANDAS/PANS. These groups can offer practical advice, emotional support, and the invaluable reassurance that you're not alone in this experience.

Local support groups may be harder to find but can provide in-person connections and practical assistance like childcare exchanges or meal trains during difficult periods. Some families start their own local groups when none exist in their area.

Extended family and friends may struggle to understand PANDAS/PANS, particularly in the beginning when everyone is learning about the condition. Some relationships strengthen through crisis, while others may become strained by the ongoing stress and changed family dynamics.

Educating your support network helps maintain important relationships and ensures you have understanding people to turn to during crises. Sharing reputable information about PANDAS/PANS and explaining how the condition affects your family can help others provide appropriate support.

Professional support networks - including medical providers, therapists, and educational advocates - become part of your extended support system. Building positive relationships with these professionals ensures better care and advocacy for your child.

Faith communities can provide spiritual support and practical assistance for families dealing with chronic illness. Many religious organizations have experience supporting families through medical crises and can offer both emotional and logistical help.

Dealing with Judgment and Misunderstanding

The invisible nature of PANDAS/PANS makes families vulnerable to judgment from others who don't understand that behavioral symptoms have medical causes. Comments like "He just needs more discipline" or "You're being too permissive" can be deeply hurtful to parents who are doing everything possible to help their child.

Developing responses to ignorant comments helps protect your emotional energy and may educate others about the condition. Simple explanations like "He has a medical condition that affects his behavior" can shut down criticism without requiring lengthy explanations.

Choosing your battles becomes important because you can't educate everyone or change all minds. Focus your energy on people who matter most to your family and let go of others' opinions when possible.

Some relationships may need to be limited or ended if they become consistently judgmental or unsupportive. This can be particularly painful when it involves extended family members or long-term friendships, but protecting your family's wellbeing must take priority.

Building confidence in your parenting decisions helps you weather criticism from others. You know your child better than anyone else, and trusting your instincts about what they need becomes crucial for maintaining family stability.

Professional validation from healthcare providers who understand PANDAS/PANS can help counteract criticism from others. Having experts confirm that your child has a legitimate medical condition provides ammunition against those who question your parenting or your child's diagnosis.

Advocacy opportunities can channel frustration about misunderstanding into positive action. Some families become involved in raising awareness about PANDAS/PANS, educating schools and community organizations, or supporting research efforts.

Self-Care Strategies for Parents

Parents cannot pour from empty cups, yet self-care often feels impossible or selfish when dealing with a child's serious medical condition. Finding ways to maintain your own physical and emotional health is essential for your family's long-term stability.

Basic self-care starts with maintaining your own medical and dental care, eating regularly, and getting adequate sleep when possible. These fundamentals often get neglected during medical crises but are essential for maintaining your ability to care for your family.

Mental health support for parents may include individual therapy, support groups, or medication management for anxiety or depression that develops during this stressful period. Many parents need professional help processing their own trauma and developing coping strategies.

Physical exercise provides stress relief and health benefits that help parents manage the ongoing demands of caring for a child with PANDAS/PANS. Even brief walks or home workout videos can provide physical and emotional benefits.

Maintaining friendships and interests outside of your child's condition helps preserve your identity and provides emotional outlets. This might require scheduling specific times for social activities or hobbies, but these connections are crucial for mental health.

Respite care - whether from family members, friends, or professional services - gives parents essential breaks from caregiving responsibilities. Even brief periods of time away can help restore energy and perspective.

Couples need special attention to their relationship during chronic illness stress. Regular date nights, couples therapy, or simply prioritizing communication can help maintain partnership strength during difficult periods.

When to Seek Family Therapy

Family therapy becomes necessary when communication breaks down, family members develop their own mental health symptoms, or the family system becomes unable to function effectively. Early intervention often prevents more serious problems from developing.

Signs that professional help is needed include persistent conflicts between family members, social isolation by family members, academic or behavioral problems in siblings, or parents feeling overwhelmed and unable to cope with daily demands.

Medical family therapy specializes in helping families cope with chronic illness and medical conditions. These therapists understand how medical conditions affect family dynamics and can provide specialized interventions.

Family therapy goals might include improving communication, developing better coping strategies, addressing siblings' needs, or helping family members process trauma related to the medical condition. The specific focus depends on each family's unique challenges and strengths.

Crisis intervention may be necessary during acute symptom periods when family stress reaches dangerous levels. Emergency family therapy can provide immediate support and prevent family breakdown during medical crises.

Long-term family therapy may continue even after the affected child's symptoms improve to address ongoing relationship issues and prevent future problems. Some families find that therapy helps them communicate more effectively and support each other better than before the illness.

Insurance coverage for family therapy varies, but many plans cover mental health services related to medical conditions. Check with your insurance provider about coverage for family counseling related to your child's medical needs.

Maintaining Hope Through the Journey

Hope is not naive optimism - it's the realistic expectation that things can and will get better with appropriate treatment and support. Maintaining hope requires balancing acknowledgment of current difficulties with confidence in future possibilities.

Recovery stories from other families provide powerful reminders that improvement is possible. Reading about children who have recovered completely or learned to manage their symptoms effectively can sustain hope during dark periods.

Celebrating small victories helps maintain positive momentum during the often-lengthy recovery process. Improvements might be gradual and subtle, so recognizing progress requires intentional attention to positive changes.

Professional support from healthcare providers who understand PANDAS/PANS and express confidence in recovery helps families maintain hope. Working with providers who have seen many children recover successfully provides reassurance during setbacks.

Focusing on what you can control rather than dwelling on uncertainties helps maintain a sense of agency and hope. Families can control treatment compliance, lifestyle factors, and their responses to challenges, even when they can't control symptom fluctuations.

Long-term perspective helps families see current difficulties as temporary challenges rather than permanent problems. Most children with PANDAS/PANS do improve significantly with appropriate treatment, though recovery timelines vary.

Meaning-making - finding purpose or growth through the experience - can transform trauma into post-traumatic growth. Many families report becoming stronger, more empathetic, or more appreciative of health and normalcy through their PANDAS/PANS journey.

Stories of Transformation and Hope

The Mitchell family credits their PANDAS/PANS experience with bringing them closer together and teaching them to appreciate simple moments of peace and joy they previously took for granted. Their son's recovery led the whole family to become advocates for other families facing similar challenges.

Sarah and Tom learned to communicate more effectively and support each other better through their daughter's PANDAS episode than they had in fifteen years of marriage. The crisis forced them to work as a team and prioritize their relationship in ways that strengthened their bond permanently.

Twelve-year-old Emma's siblings developed remarkable empathy and resilience through witnessing their sister's struggle and recovery. They became more compassionate friends to others facing difficulties and developed coping skills that served them well through other life challenges.

Your Family Resilience Blueprint:

- Acknowledge that PANDAS/PANS affects everyone in the family, not just the diagnosed child

- Provide age-appropriate education and support for siblings throughout the journey

- Seek professional help for family members who develop their own mental health symptoms

- Build and maintain support networks that understand your experience

- Practice self-care as an essential parenting responsibility, not a luxury

- Focus on maintaining family strengths and connections even during difficult periods

- Celebrate progress and maintain hope while acknowledging current challenges

- Remember that many families emerge stronger and more connected after successfully navigating PANDAS/PANS

- Don't hesitate to seek family therapy if relationships become strained

- Trust that recovery is possible and that this difficult period is temporary

Conclusion

The envelope in Lisa's mailbox looked official, probably another medical bill from their long journey with PANDAS/PANS. But when she opened it, she found something unexpected - a thank-you card from her daughter Emma's teacher. "Emma has been such a joy to have in class this year," it read. "Her kindness toward other students and her determination to succeed inspire me every day."

Lisa sat in her car and cried. Not the tears of desperation and fear that had marked their lives eighteen months ago, but tears of relief and gratitude. **Emma - the same child who had once been unable to leave her room due to contamination fears, who had missed months of school, who had required multiple hospitalizations - was now thriving.**

The journey hadn't been linear. There had been setbacks, difficult treatment decisions, and moments when Lisa wondered if they'd ever get their daughter back. But here they were, not just surviving but truly living again. Emma still took a daily antibiotic and had accommodations at school, but she was playing soccer again, had friends over for sleepovers, and talked about her dreams for the future.

This is what recovery can look like. Not necessarily a return to exactly who your child was before, but often something even better - a child who has learned resilience, a family that has grown stronger, and a deeper appreciation for health and happiness that many people never develop.

Recovery Patterns and Realistic Expectations

Recovery from PANDAS/PANS rarely follows a straight line from sick to well. Instead, most children experience a pattern of gradual improvement punctuated by occasional setbacks, with overall progress trending upward over months to years.

The timeline for recovery varies dramatically between children and depends on factors including age at onset, severity of initial symptoms, speed of diagnosis and treatment, and individual immune system characteristics. Some children recover completely within months of appropriate treatment, while others require years of management before achieving stability.

Early intervention typically leads to better outcomes and faster recovery times. Children who receive appropriate treatment within months of symptom onset often respond more dramatically and completely than those whose treatment is delayed for years. This underscores the importance of aggressive advocacy for proper diagnosis and treatment.

Most children show some improvement within weeks to months of starting appropriate treatment, though complete recovery often takes much longer. Parents frequently report that their child is "80% better" after several months of treatment, with continued gradual improvement over the following year or two.

The definition of recovery itself varies among families and medical providers. Some children return to their exact pre-illness baseline, while others maintain some residual symptoms but function well in daily life. Many families find that their "new normal" is actually better than before because they've developed better coping skills and stronger family relationships.

Academic and social functioning often lag behind symptom improvement. A child might no longer have severe OCD or tics but still struggle with concentration, handwriting, or peer relationships that were affected during their illness. Patience with these ongoing challenges is essential for long-term success.

Growth spurts, stress, and infections can trigger temporary symptom returns even in children who have been stable for months. These episodes are usually shorter and less severe than the original presentation, but they can be frightening for families who thought recovery was complete.

Long-term Prognosis and Monitoring

The long-term outlook for children with PANDAS/PANS is generally positive, with most children achieving good functional outcomes when they receive appropriate treatment. Studies suggest that 60-80% of children show significant improvement or complete recovery with proper medical management (Frankovich et al., 2017).

Some children require ongoing maintenance treatment to prevent symptom recurrence, while others can discontinue all medications and remain stable. The need for long-term treatment appears to be related to individual immune system characteristics and cannot be predicted reliably at diagnosis.

Regular monitoring remains important even after children achieve stability because new infections or stressors can trigger symptom flares months or years after initial recovery. This doesn't mean living in fear, but rather maintaining awareness and having plans for quick intervention if symptoms return.

Annual or semi-annual check-ups with experienced providers help ensure that subtle changes are caught early and that treatment plans are adjusted as children grow and mature. These visits also provide opportunities to discuss prevention strategies and address any concerns.

Academic monitoring may be necessary for several years after initial recovery because some children have persistent learning differences or continue to need accommodations even after psychiatric symptoms resolve. Regular communication with schools helps ensure continued educational success.

Mental health monitoring is important because some children develop secondary anxiety or depression related to their PANDAS/PANS experience. Having survived a period of intense psychiatric symptoms can create fears about symptom recurrence that may require ongoing therapeutic support.

Transition planning becomes important as children approach adolescence and young adulthood. This includes gradually transferring medical care to adult providers, developing independence in symptom monitoring and self-advocacy, and preparing for the unique challenges of college or work environments.

Preventing Future Episodes

Infection prevention strategies remain crucial for many children even after recovery because new infections can trigger symptom flares. This doesn't mean living in isolation, but rather maintaining good hygiene practices and treating infections aggressively when they occur.

Hand hygiene, avoiding sick contacts when possible, and maintaining overall health through good nutrition, adequate sleep, and stress management help reduce infection risk. Some families find that their child benefits from seasonal prophylactic antibiotics during high-risk periods.

Family screening and treatment for streptococcal infections helps eliminate ongoing exposure sources. Some children remain vulnerable to very low levels of strep exposure that wouldn't affect typical children, making family treatment protocols important for prevention.

Stress management becomes a lifelong skill because stress can increase vulnerability to infections and potentially trigger symptom flares directly. Teaching children and families effective stress management techniques provides tools they can use throughout their lives.

Maintaining gut health through probiotics, healthy nutrition, and judicious antibiotic use may help support immune function and reduce vulnerability to future episodes. The gut-immune system connection suggests that digestive health plays a role in overall immune resilience.

Environmental modifications that reduce exposure to toxins and support immune function may provide long-term benefits. This includes maintaining good air quality at home, choosing personal care products carefully, and avoiding unnecessary chemical exposures.

Building resilience through positive relationships, meaningful activities, and strong coping skills helps children handle future stressors more effectively. Children who develop good emotional regulation skills are often better equipped to handle challenges without triggering health problems.

Advocacy and Awareness Efforts

Many families become advocates for PANDAS/PANS awareness and research after their own children recover. This advocacy takes many forms, from educating schools and healthcare providers to supporting research efforts and policy changes.

Healthcare provider education represents one of the most impactful advocacy activities because many physicians still lack knowledge about PANDAS/PANS. Families can share educational materials with their providers, offer to connect them with experts, or support professional education conferences.

School district education helps ensure that future children with PANDAS/PANS receive appropriate educational support more quickly. Many families work with their districts to develop policies and procedures for supporting students with these conditions.

Research participation and fundraising support scientific efforts to better understand PANDAS/PANS and develop improved treatments. Many families donate to research organizations or participate in studies that may benefit future children.

Social media and online advocacy help raise awareness and connect families with resources and support. Sharing accurate information about PANDAS/PANS helps combat misinformation and reduces the isolation that many families experience.

Legislative advocacy can influence insurance coverage policies and research funding priorities. Some families become involved in efforts to mandate insurance coverage for PANDAS/PANS treatments or increase federal research funding.

Professional organization outreach helps ensure that medical, educational, and mental health professionals receive accurate information about PANDAS/PANS. Many families speak at conferences or provide input on professional guidelines and recommendations.

Resources for Continued Support

PANDAS Physicians Network maintains lists of healthcare providers experienced in diagnosing and treating PANDAS/PANS. This resource is invaluable for families seeking knowledgeable medical care or second opinions.

The International OCD Foundation provides educational resources about PANDAS/PANS and connects families with support groups and treatment providers. Their website includes fact sheets, webinars, and advocacy tools for families and professionals.

PANDAS Network offers comprehensive resources including educational materials, support groups, research updates, and advocacy opportunities. They maintain active online communities where families can connect and share experiences.

Academic medical centers with PANDAS/PANS programs often provide specialized care and participate in research studies. Stanford University, Georgetown University, and other institutions have developed expertise in these conditions and may accept patients from distant locations.

Online support communities provide 24/7 access to others who understand the unique challenges of PANDAS/PANS. These groups can offer practical advice, emotional support, and connections to local resources.

Professional organizations like the American Academy of Pediatrics and American Psychiatric Association have published position statements and educational materials about PANDAS/PANS that can be shared with healthcare providers.

Research organizations focused on PANDAS/PANS conduct studies and provide updates on treatment advances. Following these organizations helps families stay informed about new developments that might benefit their children.

Celebrating Growth and Transformation

The PANDAS/PANS journey, while difficult, often leads to unexpected growth and positive changes that families couldn't have imagined at the beginning. Children frequently develop remarkable resilience, empathy, and determination through their recovery process.

Many families report that their experience with PANDAS/PANS has made them more compassionate, more appreciative of health and normalcy, and more skilled at advocating for themselves and others. These are valuable life skills that serve families well beyond their medical journey.

Children who recover from PANDAS/PANS often show increased empathy for others who struggle with invisible disabilities or mental health challenges. They become powerful advocates for acceptance and understanding because they've experienced how dramatically brain chemistry can affect behavior.

Family relationships frequently strengthen through the process of facing challenges together and learning to communicate more effectively. Many parents report that their marriages and family bonds are stronger after successfully navigating their child's recovery.

Academic and social skills often rebound to levels higher than before the illness because children have learned to work harder, appreciate opportunities, and value relationships more deeply. The determination required for recovery often translates into success in other areas of life.

Some children discover new interests or talents during their recovery process. Art therapy, music, writing, or other activities used as coping strategies sometimes become lifelong passions that enrich their lives in unexpected ways.

Career choices are sometimes influenced by the PANDAS/PANS experience, with children choosing to pursue medicine, research, advocacy, or other helping professions. These children often bring unique perspectives and compassion to their chosen fields.

Building a Legacy of Hope

Your family's journey through PANDAS/PANS becomes part of a larger story of families who have faced this challenge and emerged stronger. Every child who recovers, every family that heals, and every advocate who educates others contributes to progress in understanding and treating these conditions.

The research being conducted today builds on the experiences of families who came before you and will benefit children diagnosed in the future. Your participation in this process - through treatment compliance, research participation, or advocacy efforts - contributes to this legacy.

Future children will benefit from the awareness you've helped create, the providers you've educated, and the policies you've influenced. The path may be easier for them because of the work you and other families have done to pave the way.

Your child's recovery story will inspire other families facing similar challenges. Whether shared formally through advocacy work or informally through support groups and online communities, your experience provides hope to others who are still struggling.

The strength and resilience your family has developed through this experience will serve you well in facing future challenges. The skills you've learned - advocacy, persistence, research, collaboration - are valuable tools for navigating life's difficulties.

The healthcare providers who have learned about PANDAS/PANS through working with your family will be better equipped to help future patients. Your advocacy and education efforts have a multiplying effect that extends far beyond your own family.

Most importantly, your child has learned that they can overcome tremendous challenges, that their family will support them through anything, and that recovery is possible even from seemingly hopeless situations. These lessons will serve them throughout their lives.

Your Ongoing Journey

Recovery from PANDAS/PANS is not a destination but an ongoing journey that continues to unfold over years. Each milestone achieved, each challenge overcome, and each lesson learned becomes part of your family's story of resilience and growth.

The medical aspects of management may become routine over time, but the personal growth and family strengthening continue long after symptoms resolve. Many families find that they continue to discover positive changes and unexpected benefits years after their child's initial recovery.

Staying connected with the PANDAS/PANS community provides ongoing support and opportunities to help others. Whether through formal advocacy work or informal mentoring of newly diagnosed families, your experience becomes a valuable resource for others.

Regular reflection on how far you've come helps maintain perspective during difficult moments and reinforces the progress you've made. Looking back at symptom logs from the worst periods can be powerful reminders of your child's remarkable recovery.

Celebrating milestones - both medical and personal - acknowledges the hard work your family has done and the progress your child has made. These celebrations reinforce positive momentum and create positive memories to balance the difficult ones.

Planning for the future with confidence, rather than fear, represents one of the most significant victories in recovery. When you can think about your child's future with excitement rather than anxiety, you know you've truly reclaimed hope.

The tools you've developed - medical knowledge, advocacy skills, stress management techniques, and family communication strategies - will serve your family well in facing any future challenges. You've learned that you can handle more than you ever thought possible.

Words of Encouragement for the Road Ahead

You have been braver than you believed, stronger than you seemed, and more capable than you imagined when this journey began. The fact that you're reading this book, advocating for your child, and refusing to give up demonstrates a level of courage and determination that many people never discover within themselves.

Your child is fortunate to have parents who refused to accept dismissive attitudes from healthcare providers, who researched relentlessly to find answers, and who fought tirelessly for appropriate treatment. This advocacy has made all the difference in their recovery journey.

The worst is likely behind you if you've implemented appropriate treatment and support strategies. While there may be bumps in the road ahead, you now have the knowledge, tools, and team to handle whatever comes your way.

Recovery is not only possible but probable with appropriate treatment and support. The vast majority of children with PANDAS/PANS do improve significantly, and many recover completely. Your child can be part of these success statistics.

The skills your child has learned through this experience - resilience, determination, self-advocacy, and empathy - will serve them well throughout their lives. They are likely to be stronger, more compassionate, and more appreciative of life because of what they've overcome.

Your family's journey through PANDAS/PANS has equipped you with knowledge and strength that few families possess. You've learned to navigate complex medical systems, advocate effectively, and support each other through tremendous challenges.

The future holds promise for continued advances in understanding and treating PANDAS/PANS. Research continues, awareness grows, and treatment options improve. Your child's long-term outlook is better than that of children diagnosed even a few years ago.

Most importantly, your child is still the amazing person they always were - PANDAS/PANS was just a temporary visitor that interrupted their journey. With appropriate treatment and support, their true personality and potential can shine through once again.

You have everything you need to successfully navigate the ongoing journey ahead. Trust your instincts, maintain hope, and continue advocating for your child. Recovery is not only possible - it's happening right now, one day at a time.

Appendix A: Symptom Tracking Sheets and Logs

Daily Symptom Tracking Log

This comprehensive tracking sheet helps families monitor PANDAS/PANS symptoms over time to identify patterns, triggers, and treatment responses. The log includes:

Basic Information Section:

- Child's name and date

- Current medications and dosages

- Recent illnesses or exposures

- Stress levels (school, family, social)

- Sleep quality and duration

Symptom Severity Ratings (1-10 scale):

- Obsessive-compulsive behaviors

- Tics (motor and vocal)

- Anxiety levels

- Mood changes/irritability

- Rage episodes

- Attention/concentration

- Social withdrawal

- Physical symptoms (headaches, stomach aches, joint pain)

Specific Behavioral Observations:

- Handwriting quality

- Academic performance
- Social interactions
- Sleep patterns
- Eating behaviors
- Sensory sensitivities

Weekly Summary Template

A condensed version for tracking broader patterns:

- Overall symptom trends
- Treatment changes
- Environmental factors
- School performance
- Family functioning
- Notable events or triggers

Monthly Progress Review

Designed for healthcare provider visits:

- Symptom improvement percentages
- Functional improvements
- Medication effectiveness
- Side effects experienced
- Goals achieved and new targets

Infection and Flare Tracking Log

Specialized form for documenting:

- Infection symptoms and dates

- Family member illnesses

- Antibiotic treatments

- Symptom flare timing

- Recovery patterns

- Prevention strategies used

Treatment Response Tracker

For monitoring specific interventions:

- Medication start dates and dosages

- Therapy session notes

- Educational accommodation effectiveness

- Supplement trials

- Dietary changes

- Exercise programs

Appendix B: Healthcare Provider Questions and Checklists

Initial Consultation Preparation Checklist

Before the Appointment:

- Complete medical history form
- Gather previous medical records
- Compile list of current symptoms
- Prepare timeline of symptom onset
- List all medications and supplements
- Document family medical history
- Prepare insurance information

Questions for Primary Care Providers:

- Are you familiar with PANDAS/PANS diagnostic criteria?
- What testing do you recommend for suspected cases?
- Can you refer us to specialists experienced with these conditions?
- How do you typically treat sudden-onset OCD in children?
- What are your thoughts on antibiotic treatment for PANDAS?
- Do you have experience with anti-inflammatory treatments?

Questions for PANDAS/PANS Specialists:

- How many children with PANDAS/PANS have you treated?
- What is your typical treatment approach?
- How do you monitor treatment response?

- What are realistic expectations for recovery?

- How do you handle treatment-resistant cases?

- What role do you see for family therapy?

- How do you coordinate with schools?

Questions for Mental Health Providers:

- Do you have experience treating PANDAS/PANS-related symptoms?

- How do you modify CBT/ERP for children with brain inflammation?

- What accommodations do you make during active flares?

- How do you work with families during medical treatment?

- What signs indicate need for psychiatric hospitalization?

- How do you coordinate care with medical providers?

Emergency Department Preparation

Information to bring for crisis situations:

- Current diagnosis and medical summary

- Current medication list

- Recent treatment history

- Emergency contact information for regular providers

- Insurance information

- Copy of current educational accommodations

Specialist Referral Checklist

When seeking referrals, ensure providers have:

- Experience with PANDAS/PANS specifically

- Willingness to coordinate with other team members
- Understanding of fluctuating symptom patterns
- Availability for urgent consultations
- Acceptance of your insurance plan

Appendix C: Educational Accommodation Templates

504 Plan Template for PANDAS/PANS

Academic Accommodations:

- Extended time for assignments and tests (typically 50-100% additional time)

- Permission to use computer/tablet for written work

- Reduced written output when content mastery can be demonstrated otherwise

- Alternative assessment methods (oral testing, projects instead of written exams)

- Preferential seating away from distractions

- Frequent breaks during lengthy activities

- Access to fidget tools or stress balls

- Copy of notes or note-taking assistance

Behavioral and Social Accommodations:

- Designated safe space and person in school

- Permission to leave classroom if anxiety becomes overwhelming

- Modified expectations for group work and presentations

- Structured social opportunities with guidance

- Advance notice of schedule changes or special events

- Bathroom and water fountain accommodations

- Modified physical education requirements

Attendance and Schedule Modifications:

- Excused absences for medical appointments
- Late arrival or early dismissal accommodations
- Modified schedule during symptom flares
- Home instruction when medically necessary
- Flexible deadlines for missed work due to symptoms
- Gradual reintegration plan after extended absences

Communication and Monitoring:

- Regular communication between home and school
- Weekly progress monitoring
- Crisis intervention protocols
- Staff training on PANDAS/PANS
- Transition planning for new school years

IEP Goals Template

For children requiring specialized instruction:

Academic Goals:

- Improve written expression skills compensating for fine motor difficulties
- Develop organizational strategies for managing assignments
- Increase sustained attention for academic tasks
- Build academic confidence and self-advocacy skills

Social-Emotional Goals:

- Develop coping strategies for anxiety in school settings
- Improve peer interaction skills

- Build emotional regulation techniques

- Increase participation in classroom activities

Communication Goals:

- Express needs and request assistance appropriately

- Communicate about symptoms without shame or embarrassment

- Develop self-advocacy skills for accommodation requests

Appendix D: Emergency Action Plan Templates

PANDAS/PANS Crisis Action Plan

Emergency Contact Information:

- Primary care physician (office and after-hours)
- PANDAS/PANS specialist
- Mental health provider
- School counselor/nurse
- Close family friend or relative
- Insurance company
- Local emergency room

Symptom Severity Levels and Responses:

Level 1 - Mild Flare:

- Increased monitoring and documentation
- Contact primary provider within 24-48 hours
- Implement stress reduction strategies
- Consider NSAIDs if approved by provider
- Increase family support and accommodations

Level 2 - Moderate Flare:

- Contact specialist within 24 hours
- May need medication adjustments
- Notify school of symptom changes
- Implement intensive support strategies

- Consider short-term schedule modifications

Level 3 - Severe Crisis:

- Immediate contact with specialist or emergency services
- Safety planning for aggressive or self-harm behaviors
- Possible emergency medications
- Notify school immediately
- Consider psychiatric evaluation

Safety Protocols:

For Aggressive Behaviors:

- Remove dangerous objects from environment
- Ensure safety of all family members
- Use calm, non-confrontational communication
- Provide physical space and time to de-escalate
- Call emergency services if safety is threatened

For Self-Harm Risk:

- Remove access to harmful objects
- Provide constant supervision
- Use supportive, non-judgmental communication
- Contact mental health provider immediately
- Consider emergency psychiatric evaluation

For School Refusal Crisis:

- Collaborate with school team immediately
- Implement modified schedule if possible

- Provide medical documentation
- Consider home instruction temporarily
- Focus on safety rather than attendance

Medication Emergency Protocols:

- Current medication list with doses and timing
- Known allergies and adverse reactions
- Emergency medication instructions (if applicable)
- Pharmacy contact information
- Instructions for medication adjustments

Appendix E: Recommended Resources and Organizations

National Organizations:

PANDAS Physicians Network

- Website: pandasppn.org
- Provides physician directory and educational resources
- Offers training for healthcare providers
- Maintains treatment guidelines and protocols

PANDAS Network

- Website: pandasnetwork.org
- Comprehensive family support and education
- Online support groups and forums
- Advocacy tools and legislative updates
- Research funding and awareness campaigns

International OCD Foundation

- Website: iocdf.org
- PANDAS/PANS information and resources
- Provider directory and support groups
- Educational webinars and conferences
- Research updates and treatment information

National Institute of Mental Health (NIMH)

- Website: nimh.nih.gov
- Research updates and clinical trials
- Educational materials for families and providers
- Scientific publications and expert consensus

Medical and Research Centers:

Stanford PANDAS/PANS Clinic

- Comprehensive evaluation and treatment
- Research participation opportunities
- Provider training programs
- Telemedicine consultations available

Georgetown University PANDAS Research Program

- Clinical research studies
- Treatment protocol development
- Provider education initiatives
- Family resources and support

Columbia University PANDAS/PANS Program

- Multidisciplinary treatment approach

- Research participation opportunities
- Educational resources for families
- Professional training programs

Online Resources and Support:

PANDAS/PANS Support Groups (Facebook)

- Multiple active communities
- Regional and international groups
- Moderated discussions with experienced families
- Resource sharing and emotional support

Living with PANDAS/PANS Blog Networks

- Family stories and experiences
- Treatment reviews and recommendations
- Coping strategies and practical tips
- Recovery stories and hope

PANDAS/PANS Educational Websites

- Symptom information and tracking tools
- Treatment option explanations
- School advocacy resources
- Insurance advocacy guidance

Professional Resources:

Medical Training Programs

- PANDAS Physicians Network training courses
- Medical conference presentations

- Online continuing education modules
- Peer consultation networks

Educational Training Resources

- School district training materials
- 504 Plan and IEP guidance
- Teacher education presentations
- Crisis intervention protocols

Appendix F: Glossary of Terms

Antibiotics: Medications that fight bacterial infections; used in PANDAS/PANS to eliminate triggering bacteria and reduce immune stimulation.

Autoimmune: A condition where the immune system mistakenly attacks the body's own healthy tissues.

Basal Ganglia: Brain structures involved in movement control and behavior regulation; primary target of autoimmune attack in PANDAS/PANS.

Blood-Brain Barrier: Protective barrier that controls which substances can enter brain tissue from the bloodstream.

CBT (Cognitive Behavioral Therapy): Psychotherapy approach focusing on changing thought patterns and behaviors.

Contamination Fears: Obsessive worries about germs, dirt, or "unclean" substances; common in PANDAS/PANS.

Compulsions: Repetitive behaviors or mental acts performed to reduce anxiety or distress.

Corticosteroids: Anti-inflammatory medications that suppress immune system activity; used to reduce brain inflammation.

ERP (Exposure and Response Prevention): Specific therapy technique for OCD involving gradual exposure to fears while preventing compulsive responses.

Flare: Sudden worsening or return of PANDAS/PANS symptoms after a period of improvement.

Group A Streptococcus: Bacterial species that causes strep throat and can trigger PANDAS.

Herxheimer Reaction: Temporary worsening of symptoms when large numbers of bacteria are killed by antibiotics.

IEP (Individualized Education Program): Special education plan providing specialized instruction and services.

Immunomodulation: Medical treatments that modify immune system function.

IVIG (Intravenous Immunoglobulin): Treatment involving infusion of antibodies to reset immune system function.

Molecular Mimicry: Process where antibodies designed to fight infections mistakenly attack similar-looking body tissues.

Mycoplasma: Type of bacteria that can trigger PANS; causes "walking pneumonia."

Neuroinflammation: Inflammation affecting brain tissue; underlying cause of PANDAS/PANS symptoms.

NSAIDs (Non-Steroidal Anti-Inflammatory Drugs): Medications like ibuprofen that reduce inflammation.

Obsessions: Intrusive, unwanted thoughts, images, or urges that cause anxiety.

PANDAS: Pediatric Autoimmune Neuropsychiatric Disorders Associated with Streptococcal Infections.

PANS: Pediatric Acute-onset Neuropsychiatric Syndrome; broader category including PANDAS.

Plasmapheresis: Medical procedure that removes harmful antibodies from blood.

Prophylactic: Preventive treatment given to avoid future infections or symptom flares.

Section 504: Federal law providing accommodations for students with disabilities.

Streptococcal: Relating to strep bacteria; primary trigger for PANDAS.

Tics: Sudden, repetitive movements or sounds; common in PANDAS/PANS.

Appendix G: Insurance Advocacy Letters and Templates

Initial Coverage Request Letter Template

[Date]

[Insurance Company Name] [Address]

RE: Coverage Request for PANDAS/PANS Treatment Member: [Child's Name] Policy Number: [Number] Date of Birth: [DOB]

Dear Medical Review Team,

I am writing to request coverage for medically necessary treatment for my child, [Name], who has been diagnosed with Pediatric Autoimmune Neuropsychiatric Disorders Associated with Streptococcal Infections (PANDAS).

Medical Necessity: PANDAS is a recognized medical condition where streptococcal infections trigger autoimmune responses that affect brain function, causing sudden onset of obsessive-compulsive disorder, tics, and other neuropsychiatric symptoms. This condition requires specific medical treatment that differs from standard psychiatric care.

Requested Treatment:

- Extended antibiotic therapy

- Anti-inflammatory medications

- Specialized laboratory testing

- IVIG therapy (if applicable)

Supporting Documentation: Please find enclosed:

- Physician letter confirming diagnosis

- Medical records documenting symptom onset

- Treatment plan from specialist

- Peer-reviewed research articles supporting treatment approach

Coverage Justification: The requested treatments are medically necessary, evidence-based interventions for a recognized medical condition. Denial of coverage would result in continued suffering and potential permanent neurological damage.

I request prompt review and approval of this coverage request. Please contact me if additional information is needed.

Sincerely, [Parent Name] [Contact Information]

Appeal Letter Template

[Date]

[Insurance Company Appeals Department] [Address]

RE: APPEAL for Denied Coverage Claim Number: [Number] Member: [Child's Name] Policy Number: [Number]

Dear Appeals Review Team,

I am formally appealing your denial of coverage for my child's PANDAS treatment dated [date]. Your denial appears to be based on outdated information and fails to recognize current medical evidence supporting these treatments.

Grounds for Appeal:

1. **Medical Necessity:** The requested treatments are medically necessary for a diagnosed autoimmune condition affecting my child's brain function.

2. **Evidence-Based Care:** Enclosed research studies demonstrate efficacy of these treatments for PANDAS/PANS.

3. **Standard of Care:** Leading medical institutions including Stanford University and Georgetown University recognize and treat these conditions using similar protocols.

4. **Policy Coverage:** The denied treatments fall under covered services for autoimmune conditions and infectious diseases.

New Supporting Evidence:

- Additional specialist evaluations

- Updated treatment protocols

- Peer-reviewed research studies

- Professional organization position statements

Patient Impact: Denial of coverage has resulted in:

- Continued severe symptoms

- Educational disruption

- Family distress

- Potential for permanent complications

I request immediate reversal of the denial and approval of coverage for the medically necessary treatments outlined in the original request.

Time is critical for my child's recovery. I expect prompt review and approval within the timeframes specified in your member handbook.

Sincerely, [Parent Name] [Contact Information]

Physician Letter Template for Insurance

[Date]

[Insurance Company Medical Director] [Address]

RE: Medical Necessity Letter for PANDAS Treatment Patient: [Child's Name] DOB: [Date] Policy Number: [Number]

Dear Medical Director,

As the treating physician for [Child's Name], I am writing to certify the medical necessity of the requested treatments for Pediatric Autoimmune Neuropsychiatric Disorders Associated with Streptococcal Infections (PANDAS).

Clinical Presentation: [Child's Name] developed sudden onset of severe obsessive-compulsive disorder, tics, and behavioral changes following documented streptococcal infection. The temporal relationship and symptom constellation are consistent with PANDAS diagnosis as defined in peer-reviewed medical literature.

Diagnostic Criteria Met:

1. Abrupt onset of OCD and/or tics
2. Prepubertal symptom onset
3. Association with streptococcal infection
4. Neurological abnormalities during exacerbations
5. Episodic course of symptoms

Treatment Rationale: The requested treatments target the underlying autoimmune process causing neuroinflammation. Standard psychiatric treatments alone are insufficient for addressing the medical basis of this condition.

Evidence Base: Treatment protocols are based on published research from leading medical institutions and consensus recommendations from expert physicians specializing in these conditions.

Expected Outcomes: Without appropriate medical treatment, patients typically experience:

- Persistent or worsening neuropsychiatric symptoms

- Functional impairment in academic and social domains

- Risk of additional autoimmune episodes

- Potential for long-term neurological complications

Conclusion: The requested treatments are medically necessary, evidence-based interventions for a legitimate medical condition. I strongly recommend approval of coverage to prevent continued suffering and optimize recovery outcomes.

Please contact me if additional information is needed to support this coverage request.

Sincerely,

[Physician Name, MD] [Title and Institution] [Contact Information] [Medical License Number]

External Review Request Template

[Date]

[State Insurance Commissioner/External Review Organization] [Address]

RE: Request for External Review Insurance Company: [Name] Policy Number: [Number] Member: [Child's Name]

Dear Review Board,

I am requesting external review of my insurance company's denial of coverage for medically necessary PANDAS/PANS treatment for my child. Despite multiple appeals with extensive medical documentation, coverage has been inappropriately denied.

Basis for External Review Request:

1. **Medical Necessity:** The treatments are medically necessary for a diagnosed autoimmune condition.

2. **Coverage Requirements Met:** All policy requirements for coverage have been satisfied.

3. **Improper Denial:** The insurance company has failed to recognize legitimate medical evidence supporting these treatments.

4. **Expert Support:** Multiple medical specialists have confirmed diagnosis and treatment necessity.

Impact of Denial:

- Delayed treatment resulting in continued symptoms

- Financial hardship from paying for necessary care

- Ongoing suffering for my child

- Potential for permanent complications

I request expedited external review given the urgent medical nature of this case. All supporting documentation has been previously submitted and is available for review.

Thank you for your prompt attention to this matter.

Sincerely, [Parent Name] [Contact Information]

References

1. Chang, K., et al. (2015). Clinical evaluation of youth with pediatric acute-onset neuropsychiatric syndrome (PANS): Recommendations from the 2013 PANS Consensus Conference. *Journal of Child and Adolescent Psychopharmacology, 25*(1), 3–13.

2. Estruch, R., et al. (2013). Primary prevention of cardiovascular disease with a Mediterranean diet. *New England Journal of Medicine, 368*(14), 1279–1290.

3. Frankovich, J., et al. (2015). Multidisciplinary clinic dedicated to treating youth with pediatric acute-onset neuropsychiatric syndrome: Presenting characteristics of the first 47 consecutive patients. *Journal of Child and Adolescent Psychopharmacology, 25*(1), 38–47.

4. Frankovich, J., et al. (2017). Five-year retrospective review of clinical outcomes in children with PANDAS/PANS. *Journal of Neuroimmunology, 301*, 80–89.

5. Graus, F., et al. (2016). A clinical approach to diagnosis of autoimmune encephalitis. *The Lancet Neurology, 15*(4), 391–404.

6. Kirvan, C. A., et al. (2003). Mimicry and autoantibody-mediated neuronal cell signaling in Sydenham chorea. *Nature Medicine, 9*(7), 914–920.

7. Moleculera Labs. (2018). Cunningham Panel: Clinical utility in neuropsychiatric disorders. *Laboratory Medicine, 49*(2), 145–152.

8. Murphy, T. K., et al. (2015). Clinical factors associated with pediatric autoimmune neuropsychiatric disorders associated with streptococcal infections. *Journal of Pediatrics, 166*(3), 710–715.

9. Ng, Q. X., et al. (2017). A systematic review of the use of curcumin for the treatment of obsessive-compulsive disorder. *Nutrition, 38*, 85–90.

10. Raina, P., et al. (2005). The health and well-being of caregivers of children with cerebral palsy. *Pediatrics, 115*(6), e626–e636.

11. Singer, H. S., et al. (2012). Moving from PANDAS to CANS. *Journal of Pediatrics, 160*(5), 725–731.

12. Swedo, S. E., et al. (1998). Identification of children with pediatric autoimmune neuropsychiatric disorders associated with streptococcal infections by a marker associated with rheumatic fever. *American Journal of Psychiatry, 155*(2), 264–271.

13. Swedo, S. E., et al. (2012). Pediatric autoimmune neuropsychiatric disorders associated with streptococcal infections: Clinical description of the first 50 cases. *American Journal of Psychiatry, 169*(10), 1096–1104.

www.ingramcontent.com/pod-product-compliance
Lightning Source LLC
Chambersburg PA
CBHW052215270326
41931CB00011B/2360